G000294308

DESERT TREKS
from Riyadh

IONIS THOMPSON

Maps drawn by Jim Stabler

STACEY INTERNATIONAL

Contents

SAFETY AND DOCUMENTATION

The expeditions in this handbook have been collated from notes made by the author and others over a five year period of travelling about the Kingdom, from 1989 to 1994.

All distances are given in kilometres, measured on the odometer of the Nissan Patrol.

Safety Hints When you travel off the roads always go with at least one other vehicle.

- Sleep off the ground if possible. If not, sleep inside a tent sealed against scorpions and snakes.
- Use a flashlight/torch for night walking.
- Take special care where you sit, place your hands, etc.
- When accompanied by children, be constantly vigilant of them.
- Take plenty of water and, in summer, head covering.
- Tell someone where you are going.
- If you break down never walk away from your vehicle to seek help: it is too easy to get lost and dehydration in summer occurs very rapidly.
- Never take your shoes off in sand dunes as the horned viper can lurk just beneath the surface: always wear high-topped, protective lace-up shoes.

Warning When camping, avoid wadi beds during the rainy season as there is a real danger of flash floods. Be careful when driving over sabkha (the beds of ancient lakes) as the terrain can be treacherously soft under the crust.

Equipment We strongly recommend you take with you on your desert trek:

- Shade (awning or side cover)
- Compass
- Spade or shovel
- Spare tyre(s)
- Radiator leak-sealant
- Sand ladders and tow rope
- Vehicle engine spares
- Oils and coolant
- Air compressor for re-inflating tyres

(Most of these items are supplied by Mohammed al-Romaizen, tel. 465 2642)

The timings in hours given thus '**DAY TRIP** (2½ hrs)' refers to the average estimated motoring time between Riyadh's Ring Road and the site.

The compilers of this book accept no responsibility for any adverse consequences to its readers as a result of following the directions herein.

1 Diplomatic Quarter

DAY TRIP (Less than 1 hr)

2 WHEEL
DRIVE

For those who have newly arrived in Riyadh and are feeling the need for somewhere not too far from the centre of town where they can walk in pleasant surroundings, we would suggest the path which runs round the edge of the Diplomatic Quarter.

This path has been constructed from the natural rock of the escarpment and follows the contours of the escarpment, overlooking the palm gardens of the Wadi Hanifah on its west and north-west sides. It has been attractively landscaped with shrubs, trees and other native plants and in the winter months the whole area is fragrant with the scent of the acacia mimosa. The path follows a stream for part of its course, and passes ponds where the croaking of frogs is particularly noisy during the hour before sunset. At various points along the way there are well-designed playgrounds for children and small gardens with fountains and shady spots for picnics. Listen for the melodious song of the bulbul in the trees in the cooler months.

The Diplomatic Quarter is open to the public but during the week it has very few visitors. It is quite safe for women to walk there on their own.

The perimeter path round the Diplomatic Quarter.

DIRECTIONS

The main entrance to the Diplomatic Quarter is on the new Makkah Road, (**Route 40 W**), just past the King Khalid Eye Specialist Hospital.

You can join the path at many different points. Drive to one of the edges of the Quarter and walk through one of the little gardens to join the path, which does a complete circuit of the Diplomatic Quarter.

2 Dir'iyah

DAY TRIP (Less than 1 hr)

2 WHEEL DRIVE

The ruined town of Dir'iyah (or Diraiyah) in the Wadi Hanifah was once the capital of the first Saudi kingdom, the base from which the al Saud conquered much of the Arabian peninsula in the eighteenth century. First settled in 1446, Dir'iyah achieved prominence after Mohammed ibn Abd al Wahhab, the religious reformer and teacher, settled here as adviser to the ruling al Saud family and promoted the religious reforms which have prevailed to this day. In its heyday Dir'iyah had 5000 residents and 500 guests daily were fed in the ruler's palace. Revenues poured in from conquered lands and more than 100,000 fighting men were available to do battle for the ruler.

The Ottoman Empire considered the conquests of this first Saudi kingdom a threat and sent an army from Egypt under Ibrahim Pasha to destroy the power of the al Saud. Dir'iyah was laid waste in 1818 after a 6-month seige, and the ruling family captured. After Prince Mushari escaped and attempted to revive the city, it was all but razed in 1821 and all the palm trees were cut down. The surviving al Saud later settled in Riyadh. Dir'iyah was deserted until this century when a few families settled among the ruins. In the 1970s these people were relocated and the government started to restore and rebuild the old city.

Part of the Salwah Palaces, Dir'iyah.

Now the ruins rise romantically above the palms and can be seen from the highway. They are only a few miles out of Riyadh and can be visited without special permission.

Often, especially on a weekday morning, you can have the place to yourself. The palm groves around are full of bulbuls and bee-eaters.

Wander about the narrow old streets and into the ruined buildings to get an idea of the traditional design of old Nejdi houses. Rooms open off a central courtyard, partially open to the sky and partially covered by an upper storey, the womens'area, supported on limestone pillars. The mens' sitting-room, or majlis, is usually on one side of the entrance and you will see that the outer windows are so placed that a passing camel rider cannot see in.

The oldest, and possibly the most picturesque, part of Dir'iyah is the Salwa palace area to the left of the main entrance. This was Sa'ud the Great's (reigned 1803-14) seat of government. These palaces were 4 storeys high and served as administrative as well as residential complexes. A bridge once linked them to the mosque on the other side of the main entrance.

To get an idea of what the town looked like at the height of its power, walk up to the highest part, the palace of Prince Sa'd ibn Sa'ud. This huge palace has been completely rebuilt, as has the adjacent smaller palace of Naser bin Saud, out of mud bricks produced in a traditional way. You can see a few of these oozing away in front of the palace. Sometimes a custodian can be induced to open the locked doors to these buildings and it is worth going inside. Beyond the Palace of Sa'd the walls and corner watch-towers have been rebuilt and you can already walk along part of the ramparts.

To your left as you approach the Palace of Sa'd you will see a sign to the Baths. It is quite rare to find a complete 'Turkish' steam bath in an Arabian town and this attests to the prominence and wealth of Dir'iyah in the eighteenth century. There are plans to restore it. Persevere through the labyrinth of rooms to the wadi side where you will find the ruins of the cool, reception room with plastered benches and then the warm room, also with benches, where clothes were removed and the bathers relaxed and chatted. Next to it is the hot room with two basins, one heated by a brick-lined furnace underneath. Water was fed into this basin through pipes leading from a cistern in the courtyard above. Donkeys carried water to fill this cistern from wells in the wadi below.

In the wadi just outside the old city an ancient well has been restored and water is drawn in the traditional way, using donkeys, every afternoon between 4 and 6 pm. You can watch this on payment of a few rials to a custodian. Turn right as you leave the entrance to the Ruins and then after about ¼ km you will see on your right a sign to 'al Dawood Farm – Popular heritage, al Swany.'

More detail on the individual buildings and a guide to the old town can be found in Stevie Wilberding's Guidebook, photocopied versions of which are usually available at the gate, from the guard. A major book is in preparation.

DIRECTIONS

There are many different ways of getting to Dir'iyah, but we feel the easiest at present is to take the Qasim Road, (**Route 505 N**) to its junction with the Ring Road. This is exit 4A of the Ring Road. Follow the Ring Road west towards Makkah. It is **Route 40 W** at this point.

Following the brown signs to Old Dir'iyah, ignoring blue signs to Dir'iyah to your right, follow this road until it narrows and comes to a broad T-junction.

At the T-junction, turn right.

Just before the bridge across the wadi, swing off right and down into the wadi.

Follow the wadi road. Pass under another bridge and immediately turn up left to park by the entrance to the ruins.

Dir'iyah is 10 km from exit 4A of the Ring Road.

3 **Al Ha'ir and the Riyadh River**

DAY TRIP (1 hr)

2 WHEEL DRIVE

Al Ha'ir is an old village beside a new town in the Wadi Hanifah. This is probably the best place to get close to the Riyadh River to observe the wonderful bird life attracted by this new body of water. The river is, in fact, the city's treated waste water which runs for some 50 km down the Wadi Hanifa until it peters out, forming lakes in places where it widens out, and creating along its banks a profuse growth of reeds and other plants . The water attracts an astonishing variety of migrating and nesting birds, particularly in December and January. We have seen grey herons, squacco herons, little egrets, a scrub warbler, a pair of snipe, lots of moorhens and large flocks of black-winged stilts. In the winter of 1992/3 pelicans were spotted and in the following year, a pair of greylag geese. It is a bird-watcher's paradise.

Do not be put off by the origin of this water: it is quite clean enough for goldfish to thrive and the only odour is a slightly chemical smell. You can walk along the left-hand bank of the river for miles. Here herons rise silently out of the casuarina bushes on heavy wings like pterodactyls rising out of a primaeval swamp and fly squawking overhead. White egrets perch in the trees. There is a certain amount of debris left by picnickers, but still unsullied spots can be found for a picnic. The right-hand bank can be reached by fording the river at the shallowest parts (by 4-wheel-drive only) and this is worth doing as it is cleaner than the more accessible left bank.

Rapids in the Riyadh River.

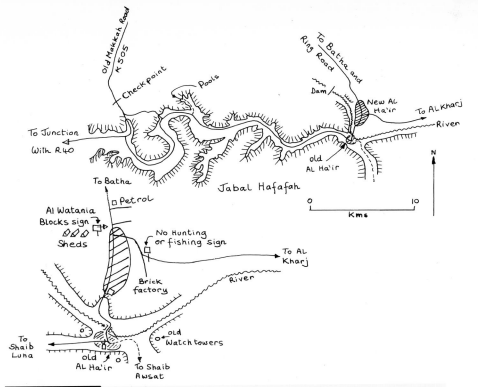

DIRECTIONS

Take the Ring Road to exit 21 for al Ha'ir. This is **Route 509**. SET YOUR ODOMETER AT **0**.

Follow **Route 509** past the new prison on your right until you reach the new town of al Ha'ir.

At the beginning of the new town you will pass a petrol station on your left. Take the third turning to your left after this. It is 24 km from the Ring Road. On the opposite side of the road at this point is a row of sheds. (To reach this turning, of course, you need to continue as far as the next break in the central reservation, do a U-turn and return to the same point.) RE-SET YOUR ODOMETER AT **0**.

Follow the road for 1.75 km , bending sharply to the right after one km, until, just before a brick factory which lies directly ahead, you turn left at a large black and white sign. This used to warn against hunting and fishing but, as it has recently been defaced, this is now difficult to read.

At 6.3 km the river appears below you to the right.

At 8.4 km you pass a bird-ringing project. Soon after that you will see several places where you can easily approach the river in 2 wheel-drive and park. You can walk along the left-hand bank of the river for some way.

4 Acacia Valley and the Edge of the World

DAY TRIP (2½ hrs)

4 WHEEL DRIVE

The thick green line of trees along Acacia Valley have made this a very popular picnic spot, especially after rain, when you will find the wadi full of flowers and flowering shrubs, butterflies, lizards, dragonflies, and birds . A wadi spur leads off the main valley to the edge of the escarpment. Here the cliffs drop away giving spendid views over the plain below. Edge of the World, a rock- framed 'window' in the escarpment, is one such point: here the drop is dramatic and sudden but there are other places where the vista is even better.

Acacia Valley is part of the old Darb al Hijaz, which ran between Nejd and the Hijaz, using the course of the Wadi Hanifah to cut through the Tuwaiq escarpment. Darb means way and this route was used for centuries by travellers moving east-west across Arabia. Ibrahim Pasha came this way when he moved to attack and destroy Dir'iyah in 1818. For centuries there have been settlements along the bed of the Wadi Hanifah and the valley has always been heavily cultivated. You can still see, on the rock terraces above the villages, the round stone watch-towers which used to guard the approaches. One of these settlements, al Uyanah (sometimes Ayenah, or Oyaynah), was the home of Mohammed ibn Abd al Wahhab, the religious reformer, who was born there in 1705. The valley is still a rich agricultural area today: fields of fruit and vegetables line the road which runs through the villages.

In Acacia Valley itself you will come across a number of small encampments near the start of the wadi and a certain amount of rubbish, which can deter the picnicker. Take one of the side wadis, such as the one leading to Edge of the World, to escape this and you will find less-frequented and prettier picnic spots under tall and shady acacia trees.

'Edge of the world' – the view from the escarpment.

Sunset in the Acacia Valley.

DIRECTIONS

Leave Riyadh by turning right at the King Khalid Eye Specialist
Hospital and heading north towards Salbukh. SET YOUR
ODOMETER AT **O**. Go past the turning to Dir'iyah. The road is now
Route 535 N. At 32 km turn left towards Jubaylah. RE-SET YOUR
ODOMETER AT **O**. Continue straight in the direction of Sadus.
Go through the villages of Jubaylah and Uyanah.

At 29 km turn left on to a good track marked, at the time of
writing, by a tyre. Near the start of this track you pass a blue sign in
Arabic. You soon enter a wooded wadi. At 37 km you pass a stone
marker in the middle of the valley.

At 37.5 km. fork right on to a good track which leads straight to
Edge of the World. RE-SET YOUR ODOMETER AT **O**. You will pass
tracks on your left but you must always bear right resisting the
temptation to follow side wadis.

At 11.3 km turn right along a track which leads you away from the
trees of the wadi and into more barren terrain. Follow this track
straight to the Edge of the World which is reached at 21.9 km

Return to the main valley track. This meets the oil pipeline and
you can return to Riyadh by following this for about 45 km to join the
Old Makkah Road (**Route 505**) near Durma.

5 **Darb Buwayb and Darb Towqi**

DAY TRIP (1½ hrs)

2 WHEEL DRIVE

Two ancient trading routes through the Buwayb escarpment north of Riyadh are now tarmaced but worth using if only to reach picnic and walking spots along the top of the escarpment or down below where, after rains, pools of water collect and flowers and bushes appear. The routes (darb means way or route) used to lead to Rumah where the wells and the lush spring grass attracted herds of camels and

'Indian Head'.

their owners. The Rumah suq used to be famous but nowadays the town's importance has declined. In a wet spring the surrounding area is still covered by thick grass and vegetation fed by rain-water carried down the deeply-incised wadis from the Buwayb escarpment.

The Darb Buwayb cuts through the escarpment at the point known as Indian Head because of the distinctive profile of the headland seen as you look back at it.Unfortunately, this once favourite picnic spot is now the site of a quarry and a fence runs along both sides of the road making access to the left side difficult. You can take one of the tracks to the right which start a short distance before Indian Head and this will allow you to follow the bottom of the escarpment for several kms. The road continues to Rumah. To vary the return, take the other road to Riyadh from Rumah, past Rawdhat Khuraym (see no. 15).

Continuing past the turning to Buwayb along Route 550 you pass the entrance to King Khalid Wildlife Research Centre at Thumamah (see no. 28). The Banban sands which run along beside this road to your left are now less congested with permanent and temporary tents and invite exploration if you have 4 wheel-drive (see no. 24).

The next turning on your right is the old Darb Towqi which now continues north to as Summan. If you stop at the top of the escarpment (15 km from the turn off) you will see a deep wadi at right-angles to the road which is one of the channels which carries water off the plateau down to the edge of the Dahna dunes at Rumah. In spring it is often full of water and consequently bordered by greenery but also a popular picnic spot and rather rubbish-strewn near the road.

Returning to the main road, turn right for about 2 km, then head off right across the plain towards an attractive wadi, usually known as Wadi Khafs, which opens up before you between two conspicuous headlands. It runs back deep into the escarpment and makes a good base for walking and for an over-night camp.

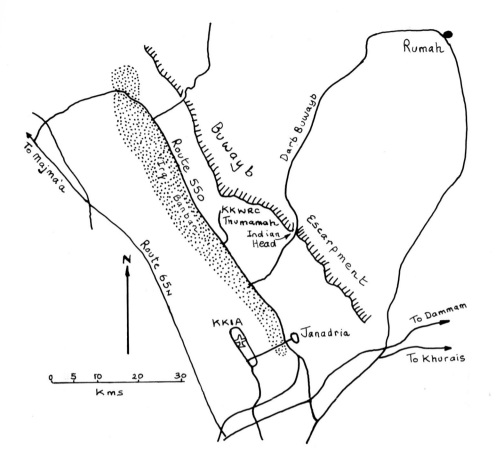

Take **Route 550** north past Janadriyah. You can join this road by
turning right off the Ring Road at the Imam University just past exit 8,
along the road signposted to Janadriyah and Thumamah. SET YOUR
ODOMETER AT **0** as you join **Route 550**. At 20 kms turn right to
Buwayb opposite a petrol station. RE-SET YOUR ODOMETER AT **0**.

At about 14 km there is a track to your right.

At 17 km you will pass Indian Head and the quarry on your left.
Return to **Route 550**. RE-SET YOUR ODOMETER.

At 11 km you pass the KKWRC at Thumamah on your right.

At 34.7 km the road to as Summan, Hafar al Atk and at Towqi is
on your right: it is in fact a continuation of **Route 550**.

6 Huraymila and the Forts

DAY TRIP (5 hrs (round trip))

4 WHEEL DRIVE

One of the old caravan routes through the escarpment, Wadi Huraymila makes a pleasant day's outing with scenery ranging from acacia covered wadi to dramatic escarpment and wide plains. You will pass several good fossil sites and two picturesque old buildings, often referred to as Turkish forts. The wadi runs east-west almost parallel to Wadi Hanifah but further north. The round trip through the town of Huraymila and the wadi and then back along the old Makkah Road is 250 km. Parts of the track are rough enough to make 4 wheel-drive essential.

You descend through a cut in the escarpment into the town of Huraymila. At this point if you look along the ridge on either side of the road good fossils of many types can be found.

The old town of Huraymila with its mud brick buildings can be seen as you pass through. This was the place where Shaykh Mohammed Abdul Wahhab first taught his doctrine of returning the practice of Islam to that of the early days of the Prophet, the doctrine later known as Wahhabism.

Beyond Huraymila is an enormous dam for flash flood water. The tarmac ends soon after this and the trees in the wadi become thicker. This part of the wadi is very well used as a picnic and camping ground. We would recommend continuing further up the track to find less popular spots.

The track cuts through the escarpment and the views down into the plain from here are spendid. You will notice that you are on a coral reef, as lumps of fossilised coral lie thick on the ground around you.

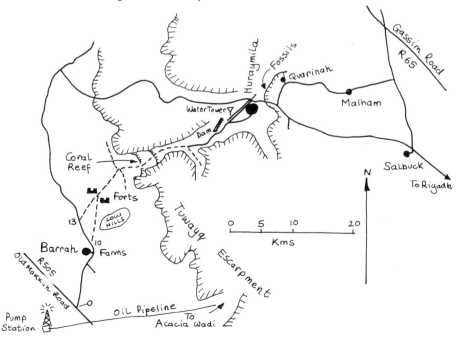

The old farm house in Wadi Huraymila.

The track then descends on to a wide plain. Just before you reach the tarmaced road the track runs between low hills on which you will notice the remains of a number of stone structures.

On the top of the ridge to your right is a roughly built stone building which might be a fort or caravanserai. On the left, in the valley bed, are the picturesque remains of a typical Nejdi mud brick farmhouse with two of original corner towers left and a deep stone-lined well in the middle.

DIRECTIONS

Leave Riyadh by turning right at the King Khalid Eye Specialist Hospital going north towards Salbukh. (At the hospital this road is signposted Dammam/Medina) SET YOUR ODOMOETER AT **0**. Continue past the King Saud University and the Dir'iyah turn-off: the road is now **Route 535 N**. At 44 km there is a check-point.

At 55 km you continue straight towards Huraymila, now signposted.

At 57 km the road bears left into Salbukh: you go right towards Huraymila. You descend the escarpment (looking out for fossils on the ridge) and reach Huraymila town at 82 km.

Turn left in the middle of the new town towards the old town of Huraymila. Take the main road straight on to the dam which you reach at 90 km. At 95 km the tarmac ends.

Take the right-hand track towards Barrah (indicated in Arabic). Follow the main gravel track until you reach the escarpment edge at 110 km. There is a good view here.

Descend by a rocky windy track on to a wide plain. The track continues down the middle of the plain. At 120 km you see the stone 'fort' and the mud farmhouse. At 127 km you reach tarmac, one mile before the village of Barrah. Turn left, go through Barrah and join the old Makkah Road at 141 km. Turn left towards Riyadh. The King Khalid Eye Specialist Hospital is reached at 249 km.

7 **Tumair and the Iris Fields**

DAY TRIP (2 hrs)

2 **WHEEL DRIVE**

The most popular of all the desert flowers which bloom in the Spring round Riyadh must be the iris, *Gynandiris sisirhynchium*. In a wet year this can be seen to right and left of the Majma'a/Buraida road going north out of Riyadh, but in a dry or normal year it is best to concentrate your attentions on the iris fields of Tumair (Tumayr), about 160 km north of Riyadh, where there is always a good show.

The reason for the concentration of iris flowers in this area is that farmers have built small retaining walls across the narrow wadi beds which cut into the escarpment to catch the silt washed down by spring rains, and form fields. These

Irises in bloom at Tumair.

fields are now mostly abandoned for agricultural purposes but the rich soil attracts a lush growth of grass and flowers, the most dominant of which is the iris. It ranges in colour from white through blue to deep purple.

It is a wonderful sight to see a field of iris in bloom in the desert, a sheet of blue. It is also fascinating to catch the moment when the buds open. This happens simultaneously and quite suddenly about one o'clock on a sunny day, later

on a cloudy one, and the magic moment cannot be brought forward by shining a torch on the buds or lighting a match near them. (We have tried this and can vouch for its failure.) If you arrive in the morning do not expect to see the flowers: if you want to arrive when they have all opened, aim for 2 p.m.

The flowers should be at their best during the last week of February or the first of March.

In a good, wet, year the variety of flowers which can be found here is astonishing. Look out for the yellow *Gagea*, the *Diplotaxis harra* and the *Horwoodia dicksoniae* (locally known as the khozama).

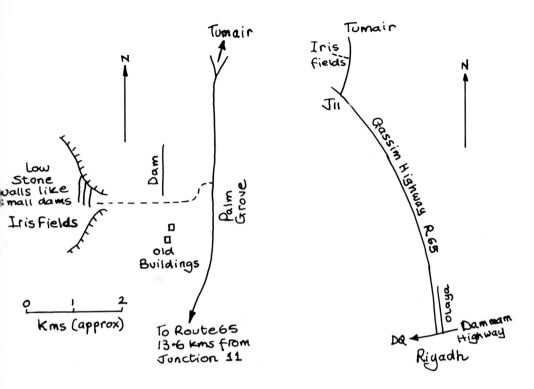

Take the Majma'a / Buraida road north out of Riyadh (**Route 65 N**).

At exit 11 turn right towards Tumair. SET YOUR ODOMETER AT **O**.

At 11 km along this road, it bends to the left. There is a T-junction on your right. The turning for the irises is 2.6 km beyond this, or 13.6 km from the junction.

Take a track to your left opposite a palm garden on your right. RE-SET YOUR ODOMETER.

Follow this track, passing a dam on your right, towards the escarpment for about 2.6 km. Look for the small retaining walls in the narrow wadi openings in the escarpment. The irises will be on the fields created by these walls.

8 Graffiti Rock I and Tumulus

DAY TRIP (2 hrs)

2 WHEEL DRIVE

All over the Kingdom you will come across rocks covered in ancient graffiti. This rock art is a rich source of information about the lives of the hunter-herders who

Graffiti Rock I and the author.

inhabited the peninsula in the neolithic period and later when much of today's desert was covered in savannah-like vegetation. They left a record on the rocks of the animals they hunted, the weapons they used, their rituals of worship and many other details of everyday life. The oldest carving dates from before the sixth millenium BC, but most of the graffiti, particularly in the Riyadh area, is from a later date. The animal and human depictions of the second and third millenia BC are often very lively. After about 1,000 BC, as the vegetation disappeared, the pictures tend to become more stylised or stick-like and are often associated with writing in a pre-Arabic script (in Nejd this is usually Thamudic). Often superimposed on this are pictures from later periods, right up to the present: sometimes guns can be seen over ancient drawings of animals which have now disappeared from the area.

Near Riyadh we have two good examples of large graffiti-covered rocks, usually known as Graffiti Rocks I and II, as well as many smaller rocks with animal drawings and sometimes script. Graffiti Rock I lies just north of the Makkah Road about 110 kms. from Riyadh. It is a distinctive flat-topped rock which stands away from the main escarpment and is visible from the road. If you scramble up towards the summit you will find just below the top a shiny black rock face covered in a jumble of figures. You can pick out a family of ostrich, several long-bodied creatures with their tails in the air which may be lions or hyenas, a human skeleton and the usual ibex with their backward-curving horns and oryx with straight horns. Several parts of the rock have graffiti on flat surfaces, so explore it thoroughly.

Then, if you walk over to the main escarpment and climb to the top, you will find a good example of the ancient tumuli which appear all over central Arabia on rocky platforms overlooking the valleys below. They come in different patterns; some stand alone while others are surrounded by ring-walls or stone circles. All are constructed by the dry-stone-wall technique and are circular. Many have mysterious 'tails' or thin lines of stones leading away from them in a wavy line which usually follows the contours of the escarpment. What makes this one unusual is that its 'tail' is interspersed with 31 triangular small cairns, so that it looks like the vertebrae of a giant dinosaur as it snakes across the middle of the escarpment, in an east-west alignment. The tumulus itself is well-preserved and looks bee-hive shaped but this may not be the original shape of the tomb. It is surrounded by a stone circle about 50 feet in diameter. All along the edge of the escarpment are other tumuli and smaller cairns. Dating is difficult but excavations of similar tumuli in the region suggest a date of about 2,000 BC, which puts this tumulus within the Bronze Age.

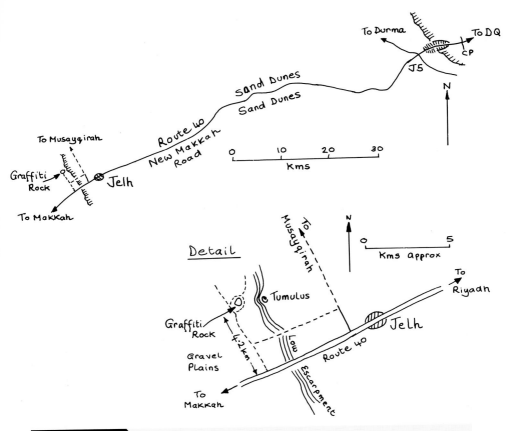

DIRECTIONS

Take the new Makkah Road west (**Route 40 W**) down through the escarpment.

At the junction with the old Makkah Road (**Route 505**) SET YOUR ODOMETER AT **0**. Continue to the exit to Musayqirah at about 77 km, shortly after leaving the town of Jelh.

Turn off right. The tarmac ends after 300 m. Continue straight, along the track which bends to the left. Follow this until you go down a small escarpment.

Then head off right on any convenient track, along the bottom of the escarpment, until you reach Graffiti Rock, which stands out from the escarpment.

The rock is visible from the road and is 4.2 km from it as the crow flies but you cannot drive straight there because a fence has been erected along the edge of the road. It is therefore best to turn off before the rock appears and follow the track described above.

9 Lake Karrarah

DAY TRIP (1½ hrs)

4 WHEEL DRIVE

The area of the Red Dunes known as Mishash Karrarah (the gurgling stream and the marsh, in a rough English translation), is a lovely place to go after spring rains. A depression between high sand-dunes is transformed into a lake by water rushing down off the escarpment along channels in the valley floor until it can flow no further, being trapped by the encircling dunes.

Flowers and plants spring up, birds are attracted here by the water and, in the lake, the fairy shrimp and other little fish re-appear. After the water dries up the lake bed is covered in a thin layer of green for several weeks and looks from afar much like a meadow. The valley beyond the lake is covered with acacia and calotropis (known locally as ushar) bushes. The dunes are like sand mountains and wonderfully red, especially in the evening and early morning light when the definition is most pronounced.

The tracks lead round the lake to a more open area and end where the escarpment meets the dunes. This rock-face has been called 'the waterfall' as water can be seen cascading down into the valley after heavy rain.

DIRECTIONS

Take the new Makkah Road (**Route 40 W**) down through the cut in the escarpment and over the junction with the old Makkah Road (**Route 505**).

At junction 6, signposted to Muzahimiyah, turn off the road. Cross to the other side by the bridge. Turn sharply right off the end of the bridge on to a track which runs along beside the Makkah road: you will be going against the traffic. SET YOUR ODOMETER AT 0 as you join the track.

Follow this track, passing a petrol station on your left at 1 km.

At 1.7 km turn left onto a newly tarmac-ed road, which leads into the dunes. At 5.1 km you will pass a mosque on your right.

At 6.5 km turn left on to a track which takes you straight to the first big lake, which is at 7.1 km. The track continues to the second lake and beyond that to the waterfall. It becomes increasingly sandy.

The approach to 'Lake' Karrarah.

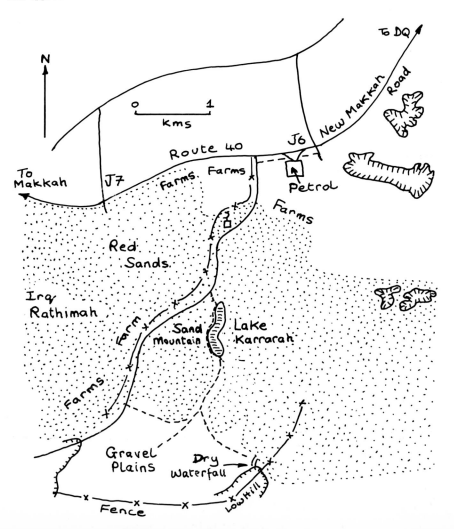

To DQ

New Makkah Road

Route 40

J6

To Makkah

J7   Farms.   Farms

Petrol

Farms

N

0   1
kms

Red Sands.

Irq Rathimah

Farm

Sand Mountain

Lake Karrarah

Farms

Gravel Plains

Dry Waterfall

Low Hill

Fence

21

10 Quway'iya and the Arabian Shield

WEEKEND TRIP (4-5 hrs)

4 WHEEL DRIVE

The town of Quway'iya on the new Makkah Road marks the join of two dramatically different geological formations. East of Quway'iya the rock is sandstone and limestone sedimentary, but at Quway'iya the north-south line of the older pre-Cambrian volcanic rock appears through the limestone. This is the beginning of the Arabian Shield which stretches right across Arabia to the west coast. West of Quway'iya the scenery is completely different from the yellow limestone and sandstone of the Riyadh area: it is covered in craggy black volcanic hills. Even the sand between the hills is different – finer and more pink in colour.

The landscape of peaky hills is dramatic and excellent for camping. The vegetation between the hills is more lush than that of the Riyadh area: there are wadis with large acacia trees, sometimes in an almost park-like setting, and side wadis with little palm gardens formed by small dams. Here you can see the almond-pink blossom of the flowering tree, *Moringa peregrina*. The rocks themselves are eroded into fantastical shapes, cones or jagged teeth-like ridges. Sometimes you may come across a hidden 'Shangri-la' at the top of one of these peaks, where water has accumulated to form a little lush meadow.

Acacia trees backed by the peaks of Jebel Hissat ibn Huwayl.

There are rich deposits of gold and other minerals in the Arabian Shield, which were mined in antiquity. One of the biggest of the ancient gold mines has been re-opened and is being re-worked at Mahd al Dahab (Cradle of Gold) south-east of Medina. Smaller mines are being explored to see if they are viable all along the edge of the Shield. Streaks of colour make the rock around the mines interesting to the layman as well as the expert: the grass-green of malachite, turquoise of copper and red of jasper. You can sometimes pick out the old mines which have been re-evaluated by modern exploration companies by following the white-painted marker stones which lead up to them.

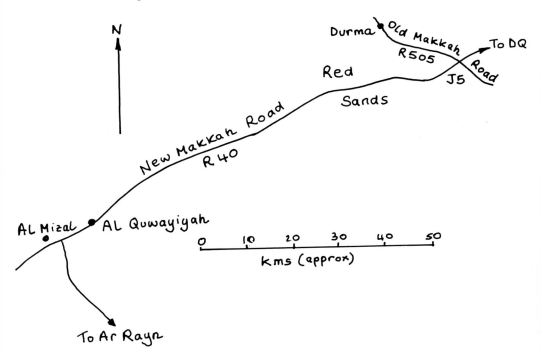

DIRECTIONS

Take the new Makkah Road west (**Route 40 W**) to Quway'iya. SET YOUR ODOMETER AT **0** as you cross the intersection with the old Makkah Road (which continues to Durma to the right).

There are two good tarmac roads which take you into the Arabian Shield scenery. You can turn left on to the road to al Rayn, about 8.5 km beyond Quway'iya, just before the village of al Mizal.

The other road, also on the left, is sign-posted to Nukhaylan, al Amar and Hissat ibn Huwayl and is 168 km from the intersection with the old Makkah Road.

You will need four-wheel-drive when you leave the tarmac.

11 Wadi Masil

WEEKEND TRIP (5 hrs)

4 WHEEL DRIVE

Wadi Masil lies amongst the spectacular black volcanic hills of the Arabian Shield, 350 km west of Riyadh. It contains a great historic rarity, three rock inscriptions in the Sabaean script of south Arabia, dating from the sixth century AD. Most rock writing in central Arabia is in Thamudic, the most commonly used pre-Arabic script in the central region. There is nothing else of comparable detail and clarity in this area.

The inscriptions commemorate raids by kings of Saba, Hadramaut and Yemen in the sixth century AD, just before the advent of Islam. Wadi Masil was in a key position on the trade and incense routes from the south .It was the gateway to Nejd. The Yemenis built 2 fortresses there to protect the trade routes and there was enough water in the wadi to supply the needs of the garrison. These forts were attacked from time to time by local tribesmen and it was following one of these attacks that the kings came north to subdue the local Ma'dd tribe. One of the inscriptions carries a date equivalent to 516 AD.

After you have seen these inscriptions, follow the wadi round its bend to the left and look up to your left at some much earlier graffiti on the rock face. There are animals and figures waving their hands in the air. One figure carries a sword and shield and others seem to have cloaks over their shoulders. Rock carvings like these are thought to date from the first millenium BC.

The wadi continues between enclosed gardens, mostly abandoned. A number of new wells have been sunk along the bed of the wadi.

Rock headland at the entrance to Wadi Masil at dusk.

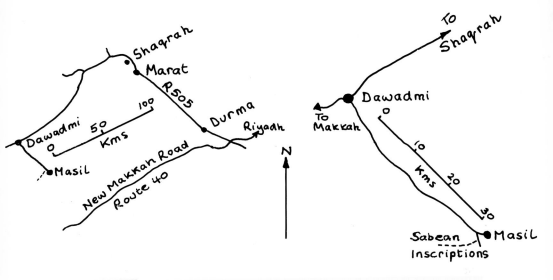

Take the old Makkah road west to Dawadmi, **Route 505**. In Dawadmi, which is 329 km from Riyadh, turn left and south in the direction of Masil, at a roundabout with a small clock tower. SET YOUR ODOMETER AT **0**.

Follow this road for about 49 km. You will see the small hamlet of Masil ahead.

Turn right about 1 km before Masil on to a well-made elevated mud road. RE-SET YOUR ODOMETER.

Take this for 3 km and then turn right on to a track which leads towards the peaky hills on your right. At this point the elevated road crosses the wide wadi mouth on new culverts.

At about 5 km you will see a narrow wadi entrance ahead of you. On the left is a distinctively-shaped hill *(see picture)*. This is Wadi Masil.

On your entering the wadi the inscriptions soon appear about 4 metres up the rock face on your left, opposite a new well.

N

0 _____ 5
Kms

Detail

Masil

Hills

Neolithic Graffiti

Sabean Inscriptions

25

12 Abu Jifan Fort

DAY TRIP (2 hrs)

4 WHEEL DRIVE

Some two hours from Riyadh, just east of al Kharj, lie the famous wells of Abu Jifan and above them the so-called 'Turkish fort'. The young Abdul-Aziz stopped at the wells here to celebrate Eid al Fitr on his historic journey to reclaim Riyadh in January 1902. Some of the wells still have water in them and are used by local people. One with a well-laid masonry lining would appear to be very ancient. As there are a number of neolithic or Bronze Age tumuli on the surrounding terraces it is not unlikely that the wells of Abu Jifan have been used continuously for three or four thousand years.

The Fort at Abu Jifan
October 1993

MCJ

The mud-built fort was almost certainly not there in 1902 and is not Turkish at all. Its style is typical of such desert forts, with towers at each corner and an impressive arched doorway. It is a large barracks-like building with rooms off a central courtyard and stairs to an upper terrace. Indeed it was used by the National Guard as recently as the 1950s. The structure on the west, or wadi, side of the fort is a grain silo for drying and ripening grain and storing it.

The fort is now surrounded by a high fence. Visitors should obtain permission to enter from the Department of Antiquities.

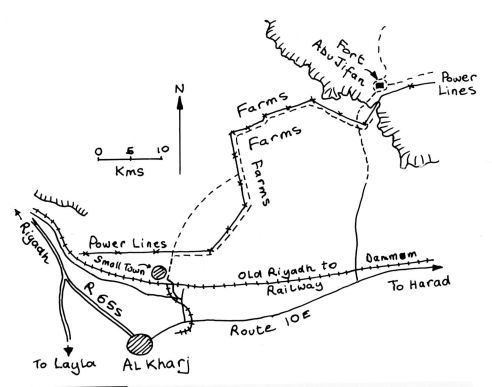

DIRECTIONS

It will take you about 2 hours to reach Abu Jifan from Riyadh. Four-wheel drive vehicles are necessary. Take **Route 65 S** to al Kharj.

In the centre of al Kharj turn left for Harad at the traffic lights just beyond the big water-tower on your left. SET YOUR ODOMETER AT 0. This is **Route 10**. Continue straight in the direction of Harad.

At 46 km turn left on to a tarmac road leading to some farms and signposted 'Hawamal Farraj'. RE-SET YOUR ODOMETER. Ahead of you are some grain silos on the left. Within sight of the main road you will cross a railway line.

After 17 km the tarmac ends but a rough track continues. It runs towards the escarpment and then turns left and runs parallel to it, keeping the escarpment to the right.

A line of electricity pylons ascends the escarpment. Either follow the pylons or take a track a little to the west of this which climbs steeply up the escarpment and takes you directly to the fort. This part of the trip is quite exciting as the ascent is steep, rutted and narrow. From this point it is 4 km to the fort.

13 Al Kharj

DAY TRIP (1½ hrs)

2 WHEEL DRIVE

The oasis town of al Kharj is worth a stop if you are passing through. You can still see the gardens and fields fed by underground aquifers which have made this an important town on the Wadi Hanifah. There are several huge farms in the area including, perhaps rather surprisingly, some of the largest dairy farms in the world. King Saud built himself a palace complex in the middle of the old town and nowadays many Riyadhians have weekend houses and small farms in the environs of al Kharj.

On the outskirts of al Kharj are the famous water-holes of Ayn Dhil where the underground aquifer used to appear at ground level through round apertures caused by collapsing limestone. Now, due to the intensive agricultural use of this underground source, the water level in the holes has dropped dramatically. Already by the late 1970s people were pointing to the ominous drop in the water, which was at that time about 50 feet below ground level. It was then still possible for local boys and men to dive off a ladder into the water and several people were said to have been swept away by the fast-flowing underground current. The water today lies about 250 feet below ground level and swimming is quite out of the question. A protective fence has been built around the edge but gaps have been made in this and at weekends visitors swarm up to the edge to gaze into the depths. Swifts swoop around the walls of the pit. Next to it is a pump station built by Aramco in the 1930s which still pumps water up and into concrete canals which irrigate the palms, but less effectively than in earlier years.

In the centre of al Kharj stands King Saud's palace, an empty concrete construction with round arched windows and behind it a large old mud brick house, part of the original complex of buildings surrounding the palace.

DIRECTIONS

Take **Route 65 S** to al Kharj.

In the centre of the town you pass a big water tower on your left and gardens on your right. Turn right at the next lights after the gardens. SET YOUR ODOMETER AT **0**. Follow brown Arabic signs to al Ayun (العيون). You will also be following a concrete water channel in the middle of the road.

Following the signs, cross over a junction and go up a small hill. The big pit is fenced off. Just below it is the pump station. It is 6 km from the lights.

The traditional Nejdi architecture of the Ibn Saud Palace complex at al Kharj.

14 **Sharks' Teeth, Khurais**

DAY TRIP   (2½ hrs)

2 WHEEL DRIVE

We've often heard our scuba-diving friends talk about their close encounters with sharks along the great coral reefs of the Red sea, but few people know that less than two hours from Riyadh by car are reefs that in their time were probably just as rich in marine life as are the Red Sea reefs of today. The visitor today is much more likely to encounter sharks along the Khurais reefs than he is along the Red Sea reefs and the fact that the Khurais sharks are 50 million years older than their Red Sea cousins makes them far more pleasant company.

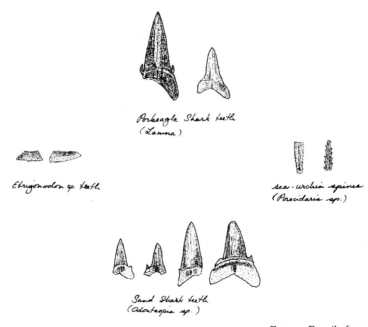

Eocene Fossils from Khurais.

During virtually all of the Cenozoic era, until about 15-20 million years ago, most of the eastern half of Saudi Arabia was covered by the sea. The thick limestone deposits visible along the Makkah road as it cuts through the Tuwaiq escarpment, and the abundance of coral and other marine fossils in the desert between Riyadh and the Eastern Province bear witness to this geological heritage. The low ridge of hills east of Khurais contains the fossilised remains of the marine life deposited in the shallow Eocene sea beds some 40-55 million years ago.

These fossils include bony reef fish, gastropods, bivalves, sharks, rays, sea urchins and other marine creatures. Of these, the bivalves and gastropods have the longest evolutionary history, making their first appearance in the Paleozoic, more than 300 million years ago.

At least four families of sharks have been identified from fossil teeth found near Khurais (sharks have internal structures composed of cartilage rather than bone, so usually only their teeth, which are numerous, multi-rowed and deciduous, remain as fossils.) The shark families identified to date include Sand Sharks, Porbeagle Sharks, Tiger Sharks and Snaggletooth Sharks. Others are probably yet to be found. Sand Sharks and Porbeagle Sharks are medium-sized sharks and are closely related, while Tiger Sharks are of course one of the most aggressive large sharks in existence today. The latter have changed outwardly so little in the last 50 million years that their teeth are virtually identical to those of their Eocene ancestors from the Khurais reefs.

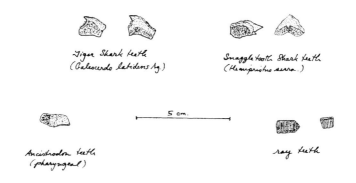

Fossilized sharks teeth.

DIRECTIONS

At exit 13 of the Ring Road take the Khurais/Dammam Road. SET YOUR ODOMETER AT 0.

At 12.5 km you pass the King Fahd Security College on your left. Take the next exit right (unmarked in English) from the main road, at 13.1 km. At 34.9 km you come to a check-point. Turn right here towards Khurais. Go through Khurais.

At 173 km you pass a pump station on your right.

At 176 km turn left on to a dirt track. Follow it for one km between low hills. The fossils are found on the flat areas, in front of the low hills.

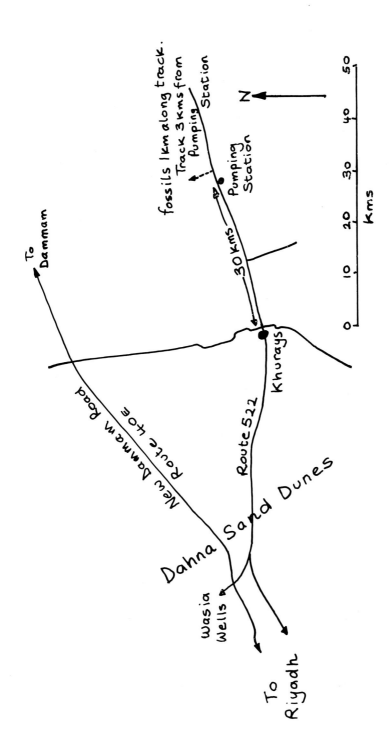

15 Rawdhat Khuraym

DAY TRIP (1½ hrs)

2 WHEEL DRIVE

Rawdhat Khuraym is the most densely vegetated area within 100 km of Riyadh. It is a large park-like area which after heavy rain is covered with a lush growth of grass, flowers and shrubs. It always has a prolific cover of acacia and *Ziziphus spina-christi* (known locally as *sidr*) bushes and these form the perfect conditions for flowers to flourish in their shade. It is an excellent place for bird and butterfly spotters.

Rawdhat means garden in Arabic: Riyadh is the plural. It is formed by the draining of rain-water off the escarpment along deep narrow wadis into a low-lying plain bounded by sand-dunes which prevent the water from flowing any further. After heavy rain a shallow lake forms and when this has seeped away or evaporated the lush growth for which the Rawdhat is famous appears.

On your way to the Rawdhat you may see the wadis flowing with water. It is very exciting to see the beginning of the flow in one of these deep channels: this is sometimes possible as you drive over one of the bridges which crosses the wadi beds.

The Rawdhat is a very popular picnic spot for people from Riyadh, but the weekdays and Ramadan Fridays during daylight hours find the garden empty of visitors.

Detail

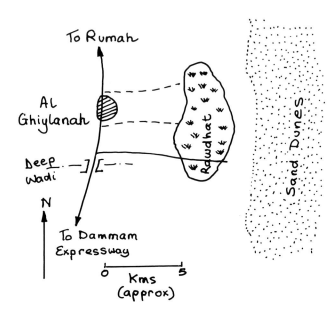

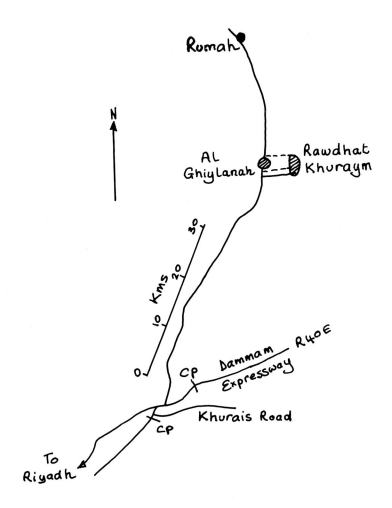

DIRECTIONS

From exit 13 of the Ring Road, take the New Dammam Highway
(**Route 40 E**) for approximately 40 km. Turn left on the road to
Rumah. SET YOUR ODOMETER TO **0**. After about 56 km you will see
a tarmac road to Rawdhat Khureen on your right.

Alternatively continue for another 3 km until you see a village on
your right.

Take the slip road on the right just before the village and follow
any of the tracks which lead round behind the village towards the
dunes, for about 4 km beyond the village. Rawdhat can be seen from
the road.

16 **Al Hofuf and the Qara Caves**

WEEKEND TRIP (4 hrs)

2 **WHEEL DRIVE**

Hofuf makes an interesting excursion, not only for its famous caves but also for its Turkish fort and mosques, one of which is said to be the third oldest in Arabia. It has a womens' suq, a camel market (on Thursday mornings) and a pottery. You can drive (it takes about 3 hours) or take the train.

Hofuf is the main town in the al Hasa oasis in the Eastern Province. It still produces famous dates and racing camels. On the east side of the oasis lies Jebel Qara which contains the wind- and rain-eroded limestone caves known as Ghar al Hashshab (the cave of the arrow-maker). They make a cool refuge in hot weather and from the roof you can have a fine view over the palm groves. Near the caves a potter makes simple unglazed pottery, as has been the custom for thousands of years.

Also on the east side of the oasis lie the remains of the mosque of Jawatha, the mosque where the first ever Friday prayers were said by the Prophet Mohammed himself, according to tradition. It is certainly very ancient, having been built in the seventh century and is considered to be the third oldest after Makkah and Medina. It is possible that this mosque housed the Black Stone after it was taken from Makkah by the Qarmathians, a heretical Muslim sect who ruled this area in the tenth century. They held the stone for 22 years before returning it to Makkah.

In the centre of Hofuf stands the Turkish fort, the Qasr Kut, or Qasr Ibrahim, with a large domed mosque within its walls, the mosque of Ibrahim. This mosque is believed to have been built by Ibrahim Pasha, the destroyer of Dir'iyah, in the nineteenth century. The fort itself was built in 1551 by the invading Turkish army. The Turks were forced out in 1680 but returned to al Hasa in 1871 and were there until expelled by King Abdul-Aziz in 1913. The oldest mosque still in use in Hofuf is the al Jabri mosque, built in the sixteenth century, which is near the Qasr Ibrahim.

Qasr Kut, or the fort of Ibrahim, built by the Ottomans in the sixteenth century.

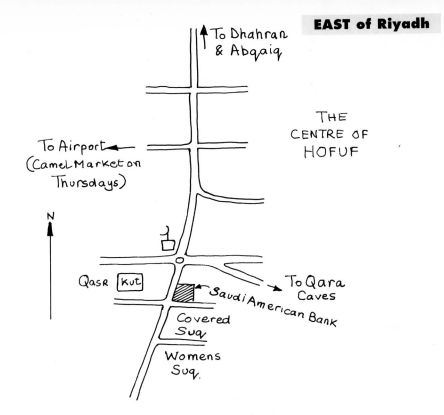

To Dhahran & Abqaiq

THE CENTRE OF HOFUF

To Airport (Camel Market on Thursdays)

N

Qasr Kut

Saudi American Bank

To Qara Caves

Covered Suq

Womens Suq

DIRECTIONS

From the centre of Hofuf take the main road east following signs for the Eastern Oasis or Eastern Villages and Munaizilah. SET YOUR ODOMETER AT **0**. One possible starting road is al Khudood St.

The main road becomes a dual carriageway on the edge of town. Go past large palm plantations on the left and a cement factory on the right. About 7 km from the town centre turn left signposted to al Mansourah.

Almost immediately you can see the low flat-topped limestone outcrop of Jebel al Qara off to the right.

Go through Mansourah. In the next village, at a small roundabout, keep right if you want to go first to the caves and keep left for the pottery. The road makes a ring round the jebel, bringing you back to the roundabout whichever way you go. SET YOUR ODOMETER AT **0**.

The entrance to the caves is on the left, about 2 km from the roundabout. The Jawatha Mosque is to be found in a sandy area known as al Qilabiya, near the villages of Miqdam and Halayla. It is in a walled enclosure, near a modern park with trees.

17 Al Uqair

WEEKEND TRIP (4-5 hrs)

2 WHEEL DRIVE

Al Uqair is an ancient port on the Kingdom's eastern seaboard. Opposite is a long flat peninsula where camping and bathing are possible and this makes a pleasant weekend's excursion from Riyadh.

Al Uqair (also spelt Ugayr) was the ancient seaport of the al Hasa region. A Turkish fort was built there in the sixteenth century. In the seventeenth century it served as the first Saudi state's outlet to the sea. After it fell again into Turkish hands in 1871, with the entire al Hasa region, the local tribesmen made the road from Uqair to Hofuf notorious by extorting protection money from merchants travelling this route. It was in Uqair in 1922 that the borders of the new kingdom with its neighbours, Kuwait and Iraq, were established, at the Uqair Conference. In the early days of the Kingdom it was the landing stage for all those arriving in Saudi Arabia by sea from the east. Now this historic place is largely abandoned except by coast-guards. There is an old fort overlooking the sea, for which permission to visit must be obtained from the Antiquities Department. Buildings along the sea front with arched windows are a reminder of Uqair's past.

The road to Uqair is lined with palms under which it is pleasant to picnic or camp in view of the sea behind but hidden from the road by the palms. Better camping, however, can be found on the long peninsula which runs parallel to the coast opposite Uqair. Here you can wallow or swim in the warm, shallow waters. Local picnickers love this area but you can find a private spot quite easily down towards the narrower end of the peninsula. Here warning notices and coastguards forbid you to camp on the seaward side but it is permitted on the other shore facing the mainland. The water here is clear and blue and, apparently, very safe, though we have seen one or two large blue jellyfish, rather splendid creatures. It is also possible, though unlikely, that you will meet the Arabian Gulf's venomous sea-snake. This is unaggressive and, as long as you are aware of the danger of handling it, there is no need to be alarmed. The ground underfoot is soft and seems to be largely composed of shells. It is an excellent place for bird-watching and fishing. Herons, curlews and even flamingos have been sighted here. You might be lucky enough to see a porpoise or turtle. It is a good place for wind-surfing but not for snorkelling.

Bathing near al Uqair.

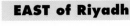

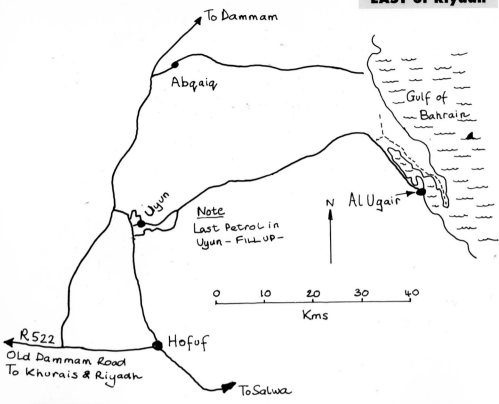

To Dammam

Abqaiq

Gulf of Bahrain

Uyun

N   Al Uqair

Note
Last Petrol in
Uyun — FILL UP —

0   10   20   30   40

Kms

R522
Old Dammam Road
To Khurais & Riyadh

Hofuf

To Salwa

DIRECTIONS

At exit 13 of the Ring Road take the Dammam/Khurais Road. SET YOUR ODOMETER AT **O**. At 12.5 km you pass the King Fahd Security College on your left. Take the next exit right (unmarked in English), from the main road, at 13.1 km.

At 34.9 km, at the check-point, turn right in the direction of Khurais.

Branch off to the left before Hofuf on the Abqaiq road going north. SET YOUR ODOMETER AT **O**.

Turn right after about 25 km, towards Uyun and Hofuf.

Before Uyun turn left to Uqair, which is signposted, and fill up at the petrol station here. RE-SET YOUR ODOMETER AT **O**.

Follow the road for about 70 km. When you see the sea, just before the road bends to the right to follow the coast to Uqair, turn off the road to the left.

Follow the track round the edge of the inlet and turn right on to the peninsula.

This destination is 4 or 5 hours drive from Riyadh.

18 Wadi Atshanta al Jafi

DAY TRIP (1 hr)

4 WHEEL
DRIVE

This wadi is one of the deep channels incised by spring water rushing down from the Tuwaiq escarpment towards the sands of the Dahna dunes. After rains the wadi channel widens and forms pools of water and grass, and plants and bushes quickly spring up along its edges.

It is part of the old route from Riyadh to the wells south of Rumah at the edge of the Dahna dunes and it was much used by Bedouin with their flocks of sheep and camels. You can still see evidence of their passing in the ancient tumuli which line the higher terraces above the valley bed and in more modern, rougher burials on the lower slopes, just out of reach of flood water.

Wadi al Jafi is rich in fossils, especially oysters, urchins and ammonites, dating from the Upper Cretaceous, about 100 million years ago. It is a good place for bird-watching: we have seen a lanner falcon in early December and flocks of hypocolius.

Wadi Atshanta al Jafi.

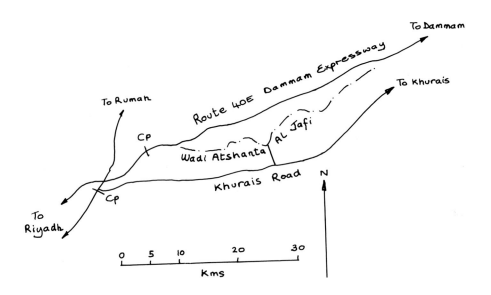

At exit 13 of the Ring Road take the Dammam/Khurais road SET YOUR ODOMETER AT **O**. At 12.5 km you pass the King Fahd Security College on your left. Take the next exit right (unmarked in English), from the main road, at 13.1 km.

At 34.9 km you reach a check-point. Turn right towards Khurais.

At 67 km, just past a blue sign indicating Khurais 82 km look for a small green tree on your right opposite a small tarmac road on your left leading to a construction site.

Take this road for 5 km until the tarmac ends. The wadi is in front of you. Turn right on to a good track and follow the wadi bed past some rock crushers and as far as you like (see Regional Map, Riyadh Area Eastern, for more detailed directions).

19 **Camel Trails and Dam**

DAY TRIP (1½ hrs)

2 WHEEL DRIVE (Trails 1 & 2) **4 WHEEL DRIVE** (Trail 3)

There are at least three tracks up the Tuwaiq escarpment west of Riyadh made in ancient times to ease the movement of camel caravans bearing traders and pilgrims east-west across the peninsula. The town of Durma at the foot of the escarpment was known to have had a flourishing suq in the ninth century AD. From there travellers needed a route up the escarpment to reach the settlements in the Wadi Hanifah. The tracks follow natural water courses but have small man- made retaining walls and, in places, steps made of slabs of rock.

We have called the track which starts to the left of the new Makkah Road coming from Riyadh the First Camel Trail. This is the best known of the three and you will normally find other people there at weekends. The tracks which lie to the right of the Makkah Road we have referred to as the Second and Third Camel Trails, in the order they are reached from the road. Each trail makes an attractive walk suitable for an afternoon's outing and accessible by 2 wheel- drive, but take care on the Second as the lower sections have been washed away. The Third has perhaps the best views and can be walked easily both ways but is difficult to find from the top. After rain a spectacular waterfall cascades over the top of the escarpment beside this trail.

On the top of the escarpment near the start of the trails, good examples of neolithic or Bronze Age circular tombs can be seen. Near the First Camel Trail are two rather collapsed circular tombs with a stone 'tail' leading away along the edge of the escarpment. About one km from the top of the Second Trail you will pass a good example of a circular tomb built like a dry-stone wall with upright slabs at intervals. The start of the Third Trail is marked by two circular tumuli and to reach these you pass through what appears to be a wall but is probably the 'tail' of another circular tumulus.

The so-called 'Camel Trail' routes up the Tuwaiq escarpment offer today's visitors several features of interest – from ancient stone steps to Bronze Age tumuli.

Not far from the First Camel Trail at the top of the escarpment are the remains of an ancient dam. The two side walls remain, 20 feet high and about 20 feet across at the bottom. The construction is of dressed stone filled with rubble. The date of this dam is uncertain and also its purpose: it may have served to create a reservoir for camel caravans using the tracks up the escarpment.

DIRECTIONS

To the Camel Trails from the top

Take the new Makkah Road west (**Route 40 W**). SET YOUR ODOMETER AT **0** as you go past the main entrance to the Diplomatic Quarter. At 29 km go through the check-point. Pass 2 solar panels. As the road starts to descend, just before it bends left, turn right on to a track at 31.5 km. Go through an earth bund and take the left fork. When the track next divides take the right fork heading for a fence. At 32.9 km go through a gate in the fence.

At 38.9 km the *Second Camel Trail* is visible on your left winding down the escarpment. (On your right is a gap in the fence with a blue sign.) From here on, 4 WHEEL-DRIVE only.

At 41.2 km go through the fence again heading towards a row of pylons. The track runs along beside these pylons which are all numbered. At 48.3 km the track has been washed away. Take a diversion to the right at this point. This is at pylon no. 79. At 51.5 km, by pylon no. 87, you are 1.5 km from the *Third Camel Trail*. Turn left off the track and, bearing slightly right, head for a gap between two low stone walls. Go through the gap and continue parallel to the main track for 200 m. Then bear off to the left, heading for a large circular ancient stone structure. Follow the track which passes to the right of this. Behind it lies a more tumbled tomb with a small modern cairn, or pyramid of stones, on top of it. Behind this is a small tree at the very edge of the escarpment. This marks the point where the Third Trail starts, but it is not visible until you look over the edge of the escarpment.

Return to the road. RE-SET YOUR ODOMETER. Continue down the escarpment to the junction with the old Makkah Road. Come off at the second exit, turn right onto **Route 40**, in the direction you have just come from. SET YOUR ODOMETER AT **0** as you join the highway. At 8 km take the first tarmac road to your right. This leads to a collection of dumped cars. There a track can be seen going off to the left. Follow this track to the edge of the escarpment where you will see the *First Camel Trail* zigzagging down the escarpment to the right. It is no longer possible to approach this Camel Trail from the bottom.

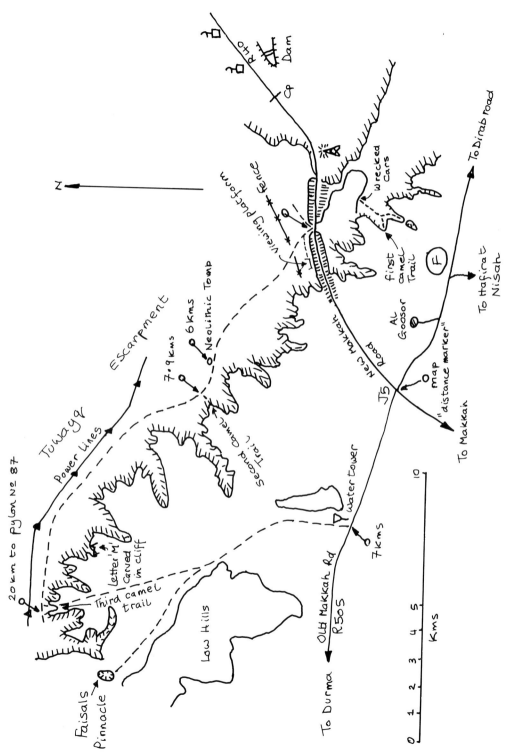

SOUTH of Riyadh

N

20 km to Pylon Nº 87

Tuwayq Escarpment

Power Lines

Letter 'M' Carved in cliff

Third camel trail

Faisals Pinnacle

Low Hills

Second Camel Trail

Neolithic Tomb

6 kms

7.9 kms

Viewing platform

fence

Wrecked Cars

First camel Trail

Al Goosor

map

"distance marker"

F

New Makkah Road

J5

To Dirab road

To Hafirat Nisah

To Makkah

Water Tower

7 kms

Old Makkah Rd R505

To Durma

Rd
Dam
g

0 1 2 3 4 5 10

Kms

42

DIRECTIONS ▶

To the Dam

From the *First Camel Trail*, return to the road and continue back towards Riyadh. Go through the check-point. At the first mosque to your left after the check-point turn right off the road and head at right angles to the road over a small rise on a wide graded track. The dam is only about 200 m from the road but is not visible from it. Take the track which leads towards the edge of the escarpment. After 100 m turn right for 50 m. Go through the piles of rubbish and you will see the dam behind and below the rubbish. If you are coming from Riyadh, at about 24 km from the entrance to the Diplomatic Quarter you will see two mosques quite close together. Cross to the left-hand side of the road before the second of these mosques, through one of the gaps in the fence which runs down the middle of the road. Go on to the service road which runs beside the main road and follow it until you are opposite the second mosque. Then follow the track as indicated above.

To Third Camel Trail from the bottom

Take the new Makkah Road (**Route 40W**) down the escarpment. At the junction with the old Makkah Road (**Route 505**) turn right to Durma. SET YOUR ODOMETER AT **0**. Continue towards Durma for about 7 km. At 16.2 km, just past a water tower on your right, turn right through the earth bund on to a track. You are 11.2 km from the trail at this point. Keeping Faisal's Pinnacle (a large free-standing pillar of rock) on your left follow the track gently to the left towards this pinnacle.

After about 7.8 km there is a Y junction: take the right fork. You are making for the next wadi to the right of Faisal's pinnacle. Enter the wadi and look out for a small free-standing pinnacle at ground level on the right. Make towards this on a very good track.

At the end of this track is the trail and a car park.

20 Hidden Valley and Wadi Nissah

DAY TRIP (1 hr)

4 WHEEL DRIVE

The name 'Hidden Valley' is particularly inappropriate for this once secluded pass between high fortress-like rocks in the Tuwaiq escarpment, now that gravel lorries thunder up and down showering the bushes to right and left with white dust. It is of all destinations round Riyadh probably the most popular with expatriates and almost too well known to mention. Everyone eventually finds his favourite side wadi off the main track: we describe two known to us below. What is perhaps less well known is that Hidden Valley leads into Wadi Nissah, a wide and lovely valley, through which you can return to Riyadh via al Ha'ir . The newly graded track up Hidden Valley makes this easier to get to .

As you drive up the dust-covered track of Hidden Valley between piles of gravel, keep to the main track with the escarpment wall to your left. You come first to the wadi known as Pinnacle Valley on your right, so-called because of the pillar of rock which stands near the entrance. This valley opens out and has good long views to the bastion-like rocks of the escarpment.

Continue up the main track of Hidden Valley. The next major turning to your right takes you into a wadi known to some of us as Teenage Camp Wadi. It has a wide flat area half-way down but the prettier part comes after the wadi narrows and the track descends to the lower level. Stop when the track gets rough, under trees, and you will have a pleasant walk to the end of the wadi.

If you continue to the end of the graded track, you join Wadi Nissah at right angles. It bends to run eastward at that point and if you turn left you can eventually return to Riyadh via al Ha'ir. Side wadis lead off the main track to the right and a few to the left. Some of these have a good cover of trees and shrubs and, in the rocks at the end, little pools of standing water where you can often find frogs and little shrimps. A good example of these side wadis is reached by crossing straight over the sandy area at the end of the graded track of Hidden Valley. This is a long, narrow wadi with a cave near its beginning. Cars can follow the bed of the wadi, which is attractively wooded, for some 6 or 7 km. After that a good 3 hour walk will take you to the end of the wadi and back, following camel tracks and the smooth stones of the river bed. If you climb up the rocks at the end you can usually find pools of standing water.

Wadi Nissah has a sandy middle which makes it unsuitable for 2 wheel-drive vehicles. It is very attractive: the red of the sand contrasts with the grey of the escarpment walls and there are lots of calotropis bushes amongst which you can often catch the turquoise flash of bee-eaters on their Spring migration. This is also a good place to see the parasitic broomrape *Orobanchae sp*. and the lovely *Pancratium tortuosum* whose white trumpet flowers open only for a few hours. February and March are the months for this.

Pinnacle Rock.

The Tuwaiq escarpment.

DIRECTIONS

Take the new Makkah Road west (**Route 4OW**) past the entrance to the Diplomatic Quarter and down the escarpment. At the junction with the old Makkah Road (**Route 5O5**) take the second exit marked Moqbil/Dirab. SET YOUR ODOMETER AT **O**.

At 5.6 km turn right towards Hafiret Nisah.

At 24.6 km you will see the track of Hidden Valley like a white gash between the hills up on your left. Follow the main track between piles of gravel, keeping the escarpment wall on your left. SET YOUR ODOMETER AT **O** as you leave the tarmac.

Pinnacle Valley is 6.2 km from the tarmac, on your right. The entrance is at present marked by tyres and a wooden shed.

Teenage Camp Wadi is the next major track on your right. It is 1O.5 km from the tarmac, and at present marked by a tyre.

Continue to the end of the graded track, 23 km from tarmac.

The long wadi described above is opposite the entrance to Hidden Valley. Go over the sandy area past a rock shaped like a sphinx on your left and into the entrance of the wadi. At 6.5 km from the end of Hidden Valley you will see a cave on your right. You can drive another one or two km down the wadi before the track becomes too rough to continue.

See map on page 46

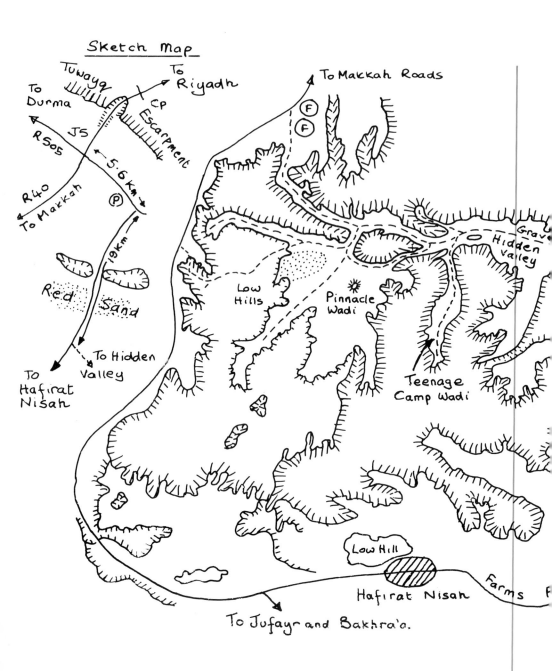

Sketch Map

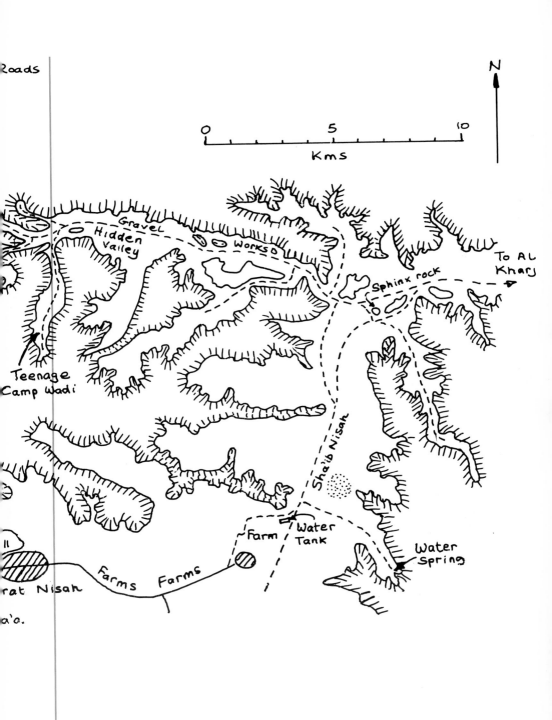

Roads

N

0   5   10

Kms

Hidden Valley

Gravel Works

To AL Kharj

Sphinx rock

Teenage Camp Wadi

Shaib Nisah

Farm   Water Tank

Water Spring

Farms   Farms

rat Nisah

a'a.

21 Graffiti Rock II

WEEKEND TRIP (3 hrs)

4 WHEEL DRIVE

This weekend outing offers a combination of sand-dunes and escarpment, with an archaeological curiosity as its goal, a black rock headland facing a narrow pass between escarpment and sand-dunes covered with ancient graffiti.

Here you will find human figures engaged in mock fighting with shields in one hand and throwing sticks in the other. One is probably wearing a headdress of

feathers, as in similar scenes found on rock carvings elsewhere in Arabia. There are ibex with great backward-curving horns and oryx with straight horns. You will see riders on horse-back and figures fighting with bows and arrows. The human figures often have their arms outstretched, the fingers and hands much exaggerated: this is a common feature of primitive rock art and is thought to represent the attitude of worship or

Rock graffiti of ritual combat.

praying. There are also a number of wasms, or tribal marks, presumably of a later date. The earliest figures on these rocks, the most faded in colour, are supposed to date from between 2000 and 1000 BC but might be earlier. The writing, in Thamudic, or pre-Arabic, script is from the Literate period, after 1000 BC.

On the escarpment behind the rock you will notice, as you descend, the tumbled remains of ancient tumuli. As was normal in central Arabia, these were placed prominently on terraces above the main wadi course.

For directions and map see pages 49 & 50

The Jebel Baloum rises prominently out of the plain.

22 Jebel Baloum

WEEKEND TRIP (3½ hrs)

4 **WHEEL DRIVE**

During the winter months Jebel Baloum, the highest peak in the Tuwaiq range, makes a nice weekend trip with a good stiff climb for the energetic, or a hunt for desert diamonds or ancient graffiti.

Baloum, or Faridat Baloum (which means Adam's apple), although part of the Tuwaiq escarpment, has broken away from the main range and stands alone. Its distinctive shape, like a flattened cone, can be detected from some way off. It is a colourful hill with layers of sulphur yellow, red, purple and cobalt blue, and around its base is a profusion of coloured pebbles. Amongst these are desert diamonds which can best be seen glinting in the late evening or early morning light, if you look along the ground into the setting or rising sun.

There are many good camping sites around the base: we usually choose the south-west side of the mountain, near a strangely-shaped rock which we call the pepper-pot (and others Cathedral Rock) because of its pock-marked surface and curious wind-eroded shape. Foxes and gerboas can often be seen at dusk.

On the south-west side of the hill are two narrow clefts leading into the rock face on the walls of which you will see ancient pictures scratched into the soft sand-stone. These cool and secret passages could have been refuges from the heat or from enemies. Near the hill, on the same side, you will see, on raised ground run-ning up towards a small hill, a large area of tumuli (stone tombs), within and around rectangular enclosures. This looks like an ancient necropolis and probably dates from the Bronze Age (about 2000 B.C.) Not far from here are some old wells sunk into the ground: be careful not to fall into these if you are approaching at twilight.

The summit of Baloum is 1045 metres above sea level and from the top you get a splendid view all round of the valley below. The most practicable ascent is from the east side and takes about 3 hours for the round journey. Once when we were on the summit a pair of angry griffon vultures circled round our heads, their 8-foot wing span giving them a threatening aspect. We usually see crag martins swooping around the summit. Make this ascent early in the day as it can be hot work.

▶ DIRECTIONS

FOR BOTH GRAFFITI ROCK II AND JEBEL BALOUM
Take the new Makkah Road (**Route 40 W**) past the entrance to the Diplomatic Quarter and down the escarpment. At the junction with the old Makkah Road (**Route 505**) take the second exit marked Qusor Moqbil/Dirab. SET YOUR ODOMETER AT **0**.
  At 5.6 km turn right towards Hafiret Nisah.
  At 24.6 km pass the entrance to Hidden Valley.
  At 57.1 km turn right towards Bakhra'a.

DIRECTIONS ▶

At 65.1 km go through the village of Huwayra.

At 68.1 km turn left on to a graded track with a blue-and-white sign in Arabic. At this point check whether you have enough petrol to get to the destination and back. If not, continue to the village of Bakhra'a a few kms further on, fill up and return to the track. SET YOUR ODOMETER AT **O**.

FOR GRAFFITI ROCK II

Once you are at the top of the initial rise the track is closely bounded by the escarpment on the left and the dunes on the right. As the valley widens, aim for the most distant end of the dunes.

Stay about 1 km from the dunes on your right. There are a number of good fast tracks. At 20 km farms appear.

At 31 km you pass a farm with several grain silos close together and a few buildings. Keep it on your right.

Soon after this you enter a different terrain, grey and stony. At this point keep the last farm immediately on your right. Just before the fence of this last farm ends, the track forks. Take the left fork. Follow the track down over 4 small rocky ledges, like small escarpments, with several hundred metres between them. Ahead of you are the dunes. Go towards them.

After the rocky descent of the last ledge, you will see a small black headland to your right. This is graffiti rock. Follow the track on your right towards it.

It is 44.5 km from the tarmac. You may descend the escarpment by a different track and find yourself too far to the left of the rock to see it clearly. In that case, turn right on to the track which runs along the edge of the dunes and continue until you see the headland.

FOR JEBEL BALOUM

Keep to the centre of the valley. At 25 km you reach farms. The track leads between them. After the farms finish continue straight down the valley: you should be well out from the escarpment on your left.

When Baloum becomes visible on your left, standing away from the escarpment, start to gradually move left towards it, following any good track. Try not to move in close to the escarpment too soon as the terrain is broken into channels and difficult to negotiate.

Several good tracks lead right up to the hill. Baloum is about 70 km from the tarmac.

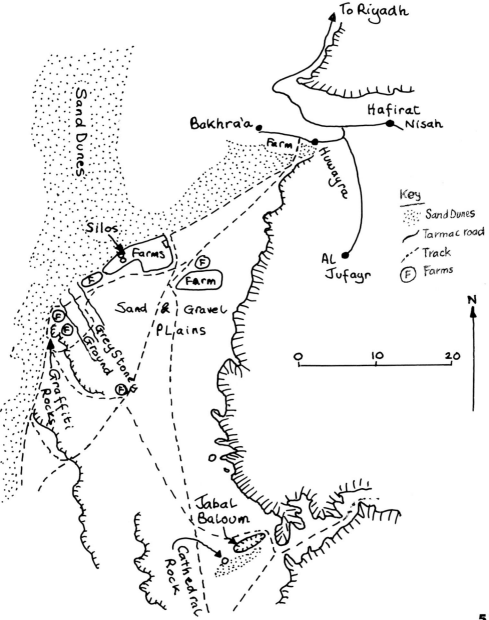

23 Pools of Sha'ib Luha

DAY TRIP (1 hr)

2 WHEEL DRIVE

Sha'ib Luha (also called Sha'ib Ha') is a green and pretty wadi which runs into Wadi Hanifa at al Ha'ir. Shai'b means wide valley. There are farms and palmgroves along the valley and sandy slopes against the cliff sides. Birdlife is plentiful: we saw bee-eaters sitting on the telegraph wires in January.

One of the pools in Sha'ib Luha.

Best of all, there are standing pools of water which survive the heat of summer being protected by rocky overhangs.They are wonderfully refreshing places to visit on a hot day, being surrounded by a lush growth of reeds, shrubs and trees. The pools are at the end of a small wadi off the Sha'ib Luha, sadly bestrewn with rubbish. To avoid this distressing sight, it is a good idea to drive right up to the cliff face (if you have 4 wheel-drive) and then walk to the upper pool. On Fridays and holidays this wadi is very popular with picnickers and during the winter holiday period you will see many tented encampments.

The lower pool, the smaller of the two, has a shoal of little fish and a constant dripping of water from the rocks above through a mass of ferns and other greenery. It is quite charming but would be more so without the rubbish which litters the water and the edges. We recommend a visit to the higher pool which is beautiful, clean and much less visited. It has water weeds but apparently no fish. Around its edges are bullrushes, trees and a mass of grass and flowering shrubs which include *Convolvulus arvensis, Asphodel fistulosus, Diplotaxis harra, Hibiscus micranthus* and *Abutilon fruticosum*. There is a hide for watching the birds which visit the pool. Above it a magnificent *Ficus sycomorus* or wild fig hangs from the rock and another stands near the edge. At a higher level still is a rocky platform with a large tree and bushes but no standing water.

Returning to the tarmac it is pleasant to continue to al Ha'ir past the farms, fields and palm groves. As you approach the town watch-towers appear on the top of the escarpment.

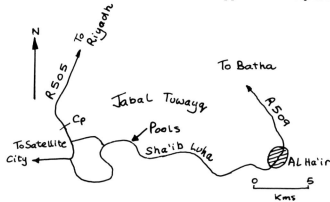

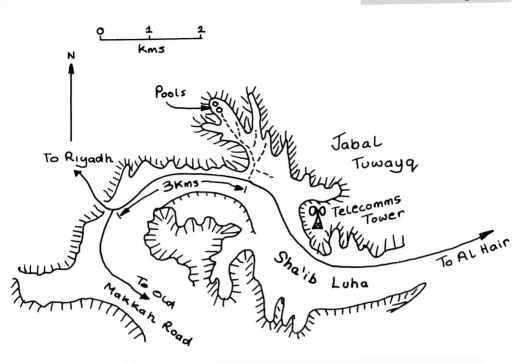

Pools

Jabal Tuwayq

To Riyadh

3Kms

Telecomms Tower

To AL Hair

Sha'ib Luha

To Old Makkah Road

N

0   1   2
Kms

DIRECTIONS

Take the old Makkah Road, **Route 505 S**, towards Dirab, passing the new Ministry of the Interior. Pass under the Ring road. The escarpment will appear on your right and, just before the road descends, there is a check-point. (This is 30 km from the Ministry of the Interior). SET YOUR ODOMETER AT **0**.

After just one km turn left towards al Ha'ir, as indicated. Go down the escarpment to the farms in the valley. A road joins from the right and at this point a wall starts on your right, the boundary of a huge farm. Follow this wall until the road bends to the right. Here, at 8 km from the check-point, turn left into a wadi which bends back leftwards into the escarpment.

Follow the left-hand track for about 1 km up to the cliff face. The lower pool (about 20 ft by 10 ft) is tucked in under a rocky overhang in the escarpment wall.

Continuing on towards al Ha'ir it is 26 km from the check-point to the centre of the town. In al Ha'ir turn left over the bridge which crosses the wadi. From here to the Ring Road is 30 km.

You will not need 4 wheel-drive, if you stop before the track gets very rutted and stony. It is easy to walk the remaining 100 m or so to the cliff face.

24 Sand-dunes

DAY TRIP (1 hr to either)

4 WHEEL
DRIVE

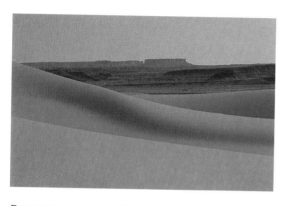

Deep russet sands are frequent features of Arabian desertscapes – as above.

When people first arrive in Riyadh what they most want to see are the great stretches of sand for which Arabia is famous. To drive about amongst these rolling hills or spend the night in them so that you see the early morning light highlighting and shadowing the sharp ridges and rounded dunes is a memorable experience.

In the Riyadh area there are several ridges of dunes (known in Arabic as *Irq* in the singular, *Uruq* in the plural).

The nearest to Riyadh are the extensive Red Sands to right and left of the new Makkah Road, the Irq Rathimah. These are popular with local residents and ex-patriates alike. Another lovely ridge is the Irq Banban north of Riyadh. This is backed by the purple cliffs of the Tuwaiq escarpment which make a splendid contrast with the deep yellow of the sands. These dunes can be reached by 2 wheel-drive but if you want to drive about in them 4 wheel-drive will be essential. Sand driving is a special skill which requires practice. Trial and error will make you proficient. You may find the following tips helpful:

- always take sand ladders and a shovel.
- always go straight up and straight down a slope, never sideways.
- if badly stuck, reduce tyre pressures to 15-20 p.s.i.
- only stop when you are pointing downhill.
- if stuck, use sand ladders; don't get further embedded by trying to drive out.
- do not drive over blind summits. Stop and look over the ridge to ensure it is negotiable.
- keep one eye on the ground immediately ahead; the other should be picking out the easiest route in the middle distance.

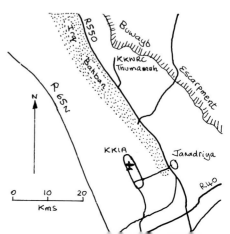

Irq Banban at dawn.

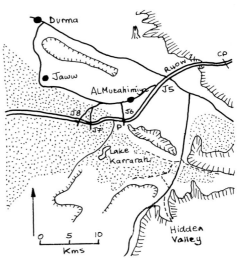

DIRECTIONS

For the Red Sands, take the new Makkah Road (**Route 40 W**) down through the cut in the escarpment to the junction with the old Makkah Road (**Route 505**), signposted right to Durma.

Continue straight on and you will see the sands to both sides of the road.

For the Irq Banban, take **Route 550** North. The sands run along the left-hand side of the road.

Pass the turning to Buwayb on your right and the entrance to the King Khalid Wildlife Research Centre. Then enter the dunes wherever you find a suitable spot.

25 Sha'ib Awsat

DAY TRIP (1-2 hrs)

4 WHEEL DRIVE

The Sha'ib Awsat is a long wide valley running parallel to and north of Wadi Nissah. Sha'ib means wide valley. It has a ridge of sand dunes running down its middle which contrasts well with the escarpment walls on either side. It is a beautiful valley and so near Riyadh that it can be reached within an hour from the centre of town. Much of the valley is now taken up with agriculture, but persevere beyond the farms into the wilder (eastern) end and you will find shady picnic spots under the rock cliffs or camping sites up one of the side wadis.

You can approach Sha'ib Awsat either from the Hafiret Nisah Road near Hidden Valley or over the Dirab escarpment. Four-wheel-drive is necessary for both. The latter route gives you the opportunity to find fossils from some of the richest bearing ridges in the area, above chicken farms. These, unfortunately, gather myriads of flies The enthusiastic fossil finder should not be deterred as an excellent trove of bivalves, molluscs, sea urchins, oysters and giant ammonites, many with the original colour and structure of their outer shells still recognisable, awaits.

This route also gives you the chance to see huge flocks of eagles, mostly immature steppe or imperial, in the sky and on the rocks overlooking chicken farms, attracted there presumably by discarded offal. The eagles can usually be seen on your left as you descend the escarpment towards Dirab soon after the check-point.

DIRECTIONS

1. Take the New Makkah Road west (**Route 40W**) past the entrance to the Diplomatic Quarter and down the escarpment. At the junction with the old Makkah Road (**Route 505**) take the second exit marked to Qusor Moqbil/Dirab. SET YOUR ODOMETER AT **0**.

At 5.6 km turn right towards Hafiret Nisah.

At 16.6 km you will see a blue sign on your right on which Hafiret Nissah is indicated and the route number in Arabic, 5395. The graded track to Sha'ib Awsat is on your left opposite this sign. Turn left on to it and SET YOUR ODOMETER AT **0**. The valley is uncultivated and rocky at first, then sandy with farms in the middle but, after the farms end, it is narrower and more attractive for walking and picnicking.

From the tarmac to the end of the farms is 29 km.

2. Leave Riyadh on the old Makkah Road heading south towards Dirab (**Route 505 S**). Go past the new Ministry of the Interior. Pass under the Ring Road.

The escarpment will appear on your right and, before the road descends, there is a check-point. (This is 30 km from the Ministry of the Interior.) SET YOUR ODOMETER AT **0**. Go down the escarpment, looking out for eagles on your left. At 10 km, just after a petrol station on your right, turn left on to a good track with fences on either side. This track climbs up the escarpment. At 16 km there will be rocky ridges on your left on which fossils can be found.

Follow the track until it divides. The left-hand track will take you to Sha'ib Awsat, which you meet at right-angles. The right-hand track soon joins Sha'ib Awsat. At this point you can turn right and after about 10 kms along a good track, join the Hafiret Nissah road.

Alternatively, by going across the sandy wadi to the escarpment on the other side, you can enter an interesting system of wadis and side wadis with numerous good camping positions.

3. Return via al Ha'ir. This route makes a good round journey and gives you an opportunity to end your trip with a spot of bird-watching by the river near al Ha'ir.

Go east through the Sha'ib Awsat until you join a graded track running north between electricity pylons. This is Wadi Ba'hyja and it runs into the Wadi Hanifah at al Ha'ir. You are 53 km from the check-point on the Dirab escarpment or 51 km from the Hafiret Nisah road when you join this track. You run along beside the river before reaching the centre of old al Ha'ir and tarmac. From here it is 30 km back along **Route 509** to the Ring Road. If you continue straight on under the Ring Road, you will find yourself in Batha, downtown Riyadh. *(See Regional map, Riyadh Area Southern, for more detailed directions.)*

26 Standing Stones

DAY TRIP (1 hr)

4 WHEEL DRIVE

Hidden amongst the hills of the Tuwaiq escarpment lies a site of ancient ceremonial significance, a row of standing stones. Surrounded by a low rocky escarpment and sand dunes it is an attractive place for a picnic. Sometimes, however, visitors are asked to leave the area by a guard, and from time to time barbed wire across the entrance to the plain on which the stones stand prevents access by vehicle. It is advisable to respect these restrictions.

The stones stand on a circular plain surrounded by low hills. They form a parabola, or wavy line (almost a semi-circle) which appears to mark the edge of the gravelly centre of the plain and the greener outer part. Originally there were more stones standing than at present: many are now lying on the ground. The tallest are more than 2.5 m. high. They have a roughly north-south alignment, so that they face the setting or rising sun. They are thought to be the remains of a primitive temple or temenos and the two rough stone structures within the curve of the parabola are possibly the bases of twin sanctuaries built to house images of the god worshipped there.

Archaeologists have tentatively dated these stones to the late centuries BC or the early centuries AD. If, however, they are associated with the stone tumuli on the natural terraces of the surrounding hills, they may be much earlier.

Standing Stones.

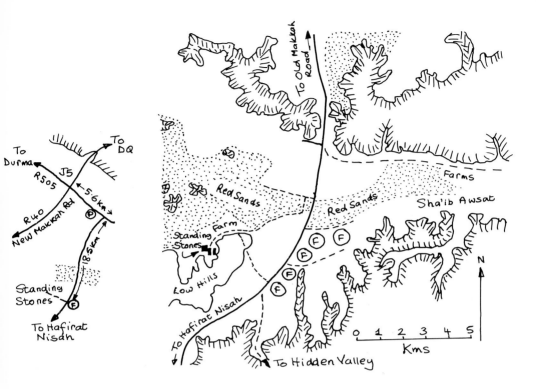

DIRECTIONS

Take the new Makkah Road west (**Route 4OW**)past the entrance to the Diplomatic Quarter and down the escarpment. At the junction with the old Makkah Road (**Route 5O5**) take the second exit, marked Qusor Moqbil/Dirab SET YOUR ODOMETER AT **O**.

At 5.6 km turn right towards Hafiret Nisah.

At 24.1 km, just before Hidden Valley, (which is visible ahead, on your left), turn right on to a track exactly opposite the end of the last green circular field before Hidden Valley. SET YOUR ODOMETER AT **O**.

Continue straight along this track passing a track which crosses at right-angles at 1.3 km and a water stand-pipe at 1.7 km. Turn left after 2.4 km, along a fence (on your right) which marks the edge of cultivated land.

At 5 km you will pass through an earth bund, which is sometimes closed by a piece of barbed wire, into a circular plain. The stones are on the far side of this plain.

27 Wadi Howtah and the Natural Arch

WEEKEND TRIP (3 hrs)

4 WHEEL DRIVE

Wadi Howtah is about 167 km south-east of Riyadh, off the al Kharj-Layla road. It is pretty enough to merit a visit on its own account: there are two villages, Hillah and Hariq, with old mud houses and wells set in palm gardens between precipitous cliffs.

Just beyond al Hillah, if you take a turning to the right, you will come to the village of al Batin, which is not signposted. It has a long main street, at the end of which, (if you bear right at the fork), you will see some substantial walls. These are the remains of two forts built by Ibrahim Pasha in about 1820 after he had destroyed the settlement of al Hillah.

The village of Hariq (which means the fire) is at the end of the tarmac. If you turn left in the middle of Hariq, you come first to a very long irrigation dam on your right, which, after rains such as in the winter of 1992-3, forms a lake 2 km across. Some 20 km further along Wadi Howtah you come to a natural feature of the escarpment, the natural or 'flying' arch. This takes on the appearance of a Greek column and capital as you approach. If you climb up to it you will see that it stands some 15 feet above a platform, from which there is an excellent view. Surprisingly there is no evidence here of early man, but about 7 kms. beyond the arch the track leads through the middle of a neolithic, or Bronze Age, tombfield with a number of stone tumuli and a large stone circle. These circles are often associated with burial areas in central Arabia, and may have had some commemorative purpose. The tombs probably date to between the second and first millenia.

You can make a round trip by returning to Riyadh via Jebel Baloum, either by bearing north at the arch or by taking the other route out of Hariq which passes to the right of the dam and then bears north.

Another 146 kms beyond Howtah the road south passes the town of Layla, and beyond Layla (18 km from the check-point at the entrance to Layla town) is the turning to the lakes, or Oyun. These used to be a popular destination for people from Riyadh, when the lakes were full of water and the margins had tall grass and trees. Now the water has sunk to 100 feet or more below the surface. The vegetation has disappeared and rather nondescript modern buildings now stand by the edge of the pits.

The natural arch.

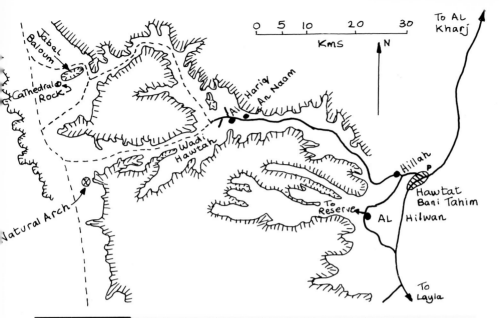

DIRECTIONS

Leave Riyadh on the al Kharj road, **Route 65 S**. Take exit 6A towards Dilam. This road becomes **Route 10 W** to Wadi Dawasir.

The new town of Howtah beni Tamim (sometimes spelt Hauta or Hota), is the next major town after Dilam. Turn right in the middle of Howtah new town, just before the brow of the hill. SET YOUR ODOMETER AT **0**. Follow the wadi bed for about 40 km until you reach Hariq. To reach the arch, turn left in the middle of Hariq at the mosque and fill up at the petrol station. RE-SET YOUR ODOMETER AT **0**. The tarmac road (which becomes a graded track for a short distance soon after you leave the mosque) bends right and continues past the end of the dam.

It then becomes a well-defined track running westward along the wadi for about 35 km. For the last 4 km or so you can see the arch on your left. Turn in towards it at about 33 km from Hariq, not before as the terrain is rough.

To reach Jebel Baloum, bear right (north) at the arch and continue in a northerly direction keeping the escarpment in view to your right. Alternatively, in Hariq continue straight, passing old mud buildings, until the tarmac ends and you continue on a track which leads into a wide cultivated wadi: the dam will be on your left.

28 Wildlife Research Centre and Ibex Reserve

WEEKEND TRIP (1 hr (Thumamah), 3 hrs (Howtah))

4 WHEEL DRIVE

Both the Wildlife Research Centre at Thumamah and the Ibex Reserve in Wadi Howtah are engaged in the reintroduction of native Arabian animals into the wild.

The King Khalid Wildlfe Research Centre at Thumamah, 70 km north of Riyadh, was founded in 1987 to care for the private animal collection of the late King Khalid, which included some Arabian species. Since then the animal collection has grown to nearly 1000 specimens and priority has increasingly been given to the native Arabian species, especially the oryx, and the idmi and rheem (or mountain and sand gazelles). These are now being bred and the gazelles are being reintroduced to the wild. The centre also does a great deal of research on the animals in its care.

The Ibex Reserve is in Wadi Howtah, 200 km south of Riyadh. It takes about 3 hours to get there. Idmi (mountain gazelle) are being reintroduced here with great success. Since December 1990 71 idmi have been released in the valley. The end of the wadi has been fenced off to protect the plants they feed on from being grazed. They have settled well and multiplied. By 1994 the total number of idmi had reached 130. The Nubian ibex, a species of wild goat, has never completely disappeared from this area and is now doing well under the protection of the Reserve. There are thought to be about 250 ibex in the wadi at present.

An ibex in the Reserve.

The animals now appear in the wadi outside the fenced area and it is possible to camp here with permission (see below), preferably in a side wadi off the main one. This is the best way to see the ibex as they tend to appear early in the morning and in the evening. You can see mountain gazelle in the daytime feeding in the wadi, or in hot weather, resting in the shade of bushes. They are rather shy. Ibex come down from the rocky slopes to feed, usually only at dusk and dawn, but as they are the same colour as the rocks, it is difficult to spot them unless they move. The best time of year to see the ibex is autumn or winter before the main rain.

Both Thumamah and the Ibex Reserve can be visited, with permission. Apply in writing to:

> The Secretary General, NCWCD, PO Box 61681
> Riyadh 11575
> (Tel. 441 0369 Fax. 441 0797)

Allow two to three weeks for a reply. A faxed application is always quicker than a letter and if you have heard nothing after two weeks or so, you can follow up with a phone call.

For Thumamah, once permission has been obtained, arrangements for a private visit can be made through the Director General (tel: 404 2527, fax 401 1527)

For the Ibex Reserve, state whether you would like permission to visit the fenced area, or to camp overnight outside it. You can also have a guided tour from the Rangers, who speak only Arabic.

DIRECTIONS

Take **Route 65 S** towards al Kharj. Turn right at exit 6A towards Dilam and Wadi al Dawasir. Continue until you reach Howtah beni Tamim (sometimes spelt Hotat or Hauta).

At the check-point SET YOUR ODOMETER AT **O**. Fill up with petrol at one of the 2 petrol stations on the left, at O.5 km and 1 km.

Continue towards Layla for about 15 km. You will see a telephone microwave tower on the right and then, after another km or two, a turnoff to the right. There is a big archway across the road. Turn right here, passing under the archway. RE-SET YOUR ODOMETER AT **O**.

Continue for about 1O km. The road goes down a steep hill, across a bridge and then there are some traffic lights which just flash away at a road junction. Turn left here. This is the first tarmaced road on your left since the archway. SET YOUR ODOMETER AT **O** AGAIN.

After about 2 km turn right at the fork. Take the first left after the fork, at about 2.5 km. You are now on a long tarmaced road. At the end of this road is an isolated building on the right.

Turn right after the building. After a few metres the tarmaced road ends. Follow the stony track. After about 5OO m, you will see another track to the left, which goes to the rangers' camp – a stone building which you will be able to see easily. You are now at the mouth of Wadi Matham.

If you are simply visiting for the day, there is no need to report to the rangers' camp. Follow the dirt tracks towards the west, up the wadi, keeping the rangers' camp on your left. Keep on the left (south) side of the wadi floor for the first few kilometres, but after that just follow the main track.

If you eventually find your way blocked by a fence across the wadi, you are in the correct place! But from the moment that you pass the rangers' camp, you should drive slowly and keep a sharp eye out for idmi.

29 Medain Saleh and the Hejaz Railway

FOUR DAY TRIP MINIMUM

4 WHEEL DRIVE

Without doubt the queen of desert expeditions in Saudi Arabia is that to the Nabatean town of Medain Saleh north of Medina and down the Hejaz Railway. From Riyadh this will take at least 4 days by car and you will need four-wheel-drive for parts of the railway.

Medain Saleh flourished between 100 BC and 100 AD and grew rich on the trade which passed through it from the incense lands of southern Arabia to the Roman Empire in the north. Its sister city was Petra in Jordan. The Nabateans were a Semitic people, formerly nomadic, who wrote in an early form of Arabic script. Their city covered about 3 square kilometres but after it was abandoned in about 100 AD the central area of houses and shops disappeared and all that can now be seen are the tombs cut into the sandstone rocks which surround the old city. These are on a monumental scale, similar to those of Petra but with more eastern influence in the design of their facades. The most common design is the stepped gable but there are also lions, snakes and roses. In the highest part of the city is a narrow cleft between rocks called the siq which opens out into a natural ampitheatre.

Nabataean tombs at Medain Saleh.

The Koran refers to Medain Saleh by its Arabic name, al Hijr, and tells the story of its destruction by God when its people turned away from His bounty. Pilgrims en route to Makkah used to turn their faces away from this city of abomination. It was first seen by Europeans when Charles Doughty followed the pilgrim caravan there in 1876 and stayed in the fort, or 'kella' which still stands beside the engine shed.

The site is magnificently situated high above the oasis. The air in winter months is crisp and exhilarating and during the week there are almost no visitors so you can have the place more or less to yourself. Permission to visit must be obtained from the Department of Antiquities and Museums (see page 74) and the permit handed to the police post by the gate.

The Hejaz Railway was built along the old Haj route from Damascus to Medina by the Turks, in 1904. They never completed the section to Makkah. During the Arab Revolt of 1916 the line was used to reinforce the Turkish garrison in Arabia. T.E. Lawrence and the forces of the Sherif of Makkah attacked and destroyed much of it

An engine shed at Medain Saleh.

Railway crossing a wadi bed.

in 1917. The line never fully recovered and the section south of Ma'an in Jordan was closed in 1924. Some of the rolling stock remains beside and on the railway to this day: it has hardly rusted. The best preserved engine stands in a shed which is being restored and re-roofed at Medain Saleh. Another good engine with wagons can be seen lying on its side at Hadiya, between Medina and Medain Saleh. Almost none of the original rails remain but you can follow the rail track along most of its embankment between Medain Saleh and Medina. This is a rough and tiring journey as the vehicles have to constantly leave the railroad embankment where parts have been washed or worn away and follow a parallel track. But it is a most beautiful route between purple jagged mountains and the interest and romance of the railway makes it a memorable experience. Take Doughty's 'Arabia Deserta' and T.E.Lawrence's 'Seven Pillars of Wisdom' for the relevant passages which make the history of the railway and, before it, the pilgrim route come alive.

DIRECTIONS

Take the Buraydah/Qasim road north, **Route 65 N**. It is 630 km to Hail and will take you at least 7 hours.

On the outskirts of Hail turn west (left) towards al Ula. You will find yourself passing the lovely jagged hills of the Jebal Shammar amongst which you can find good camp sites. It is 380 km from Hail to Medain Saleh.

About 30 km before al Ula turn north (right) towards Medain Saleh, which is 18 km from this point. SET YOUR ODOMETER AT **0**.

At about 12 km look for the sign *'To the Antiquities'* on your left but facing the other way. Turn left here. It is then about 5 km to the entrance to the site. You can camp by one of the rounded sandstone rocks to the left of the road before you reach the entrance.

Before leaving the site, drive to the station on the Hejaz Railway below Medain Saleh to see the engine in its shed and the kella where Doughty spent many unhappy days in the 1870s.

Drive into al Ula to re-fuel. SET YOUR ODOMETER AT **0**. Take the Medina road south. At about 80 km turn off right by a microwave mast to join the railway at Zamurrud station.

The attached map of the railway will give you the details of the stations. The total length of the track between Medain Saleh and Medina is about 314 km (150 cross-country). It can be done comfortably in 9 to 10 hours. A night's camp by the track is essential. The only part of the track which may give difficulty is the sandy area before Hadiya.

You rejoin the tarmac 85 km from Medina. It is possible for non-Muslims to stay at the Sheraton Hotel on the outskirts of Medina. The drive back to Riyadh from here takes 11 hours.

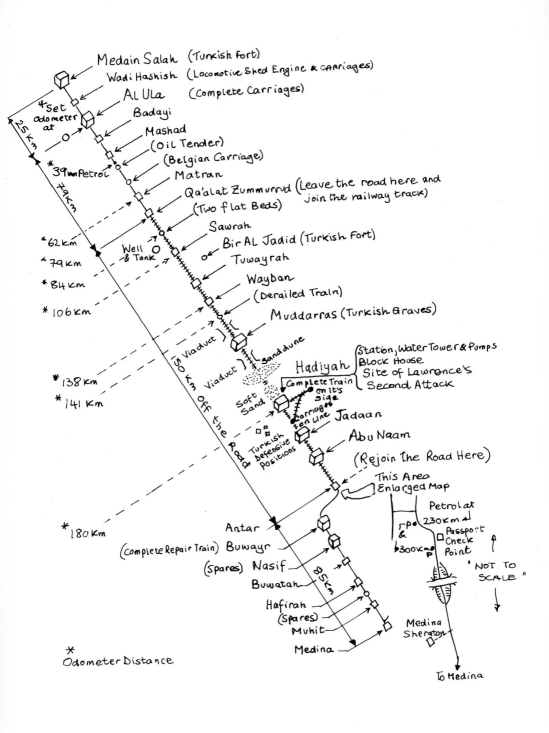

Medain Salah (Turkish Fort)
Wadi Hashish (Locomotive Shed Engine & Carriages)
Al Ula (Complete Carriages)
Badayi
Mashad
(Oil Tender)
(Belgian Carriage)
Matran
Qa'alat Zummurrud (Leave the road here and join the railway track)
(Two flat Beds)
Sawrah
Bir Al Jadid (Turkish Fort)
Tuwayrah
Wayban
(Derailed Train)
Muddarras (Turkish Graves)
Hadiyah
Station, Water Tower & Pumps
Block House
Site of Lawrence's
Second Attack
Complete Train on it's side
Jadaan
Abu Naam
(Rejoin The Road Here)
This Area
Enlarged Map
Antar
(Complete Repair Train) Buwayr
(Spares) Nasif
Buwatah
Hafirah
(Spares)
Muhit
Medina

*Set odometer at O
25 km
39 km Petrol
74 km
*62 km
*79 km
*84 km
*106 km
*138 km
*141 km
*180 km

Well & Tank
To Viaduct
Viaduct
Sand dune
Soft Sand
Carriages on Line
Turkish Defensive Positions
50 km off the Road
85 km

Petrol at 230 km
Passport Check Point
300 km
'NOT TO SCALE'

Medina Sheraton

To Medina

*
Odometer Distance

30 Qaryat al Fau

THREE DAY TRIP MINIMUM

4 WHEEL DRIVE

On the edge of the Empty Quarter south of Sulayyil lie the ruins of the ancient capital of the Kingdom of Kinda, once a huge city which flourished between the second century BC and the fifth century AD. Lying at a strategic break in the Tuwaiq escarpment on the trade routes leading from the South Arabian kingdoms to the ports on the Gulf coast and, via Riyadh, north to Tayma, Qaryat al Fau was an important entrepot and a number of fine works of art have been found there. It is worth a visit if you are in the area or making for Najran, particularly during the excavation season (currently October-end December) when you may be able to arrange to be shown round by the archaeologists in charge. (Permission can be obtained from the Department of Antiquities and Museums – see page 74.) The excavation is being conducted by the Department of Archaeology of King Saud University.

You can see the layout of the old town with its souks, temple, palace and graves, interspersed with mysterious towers. We were fortunate enough to be there when one of the graves was being emptied of its goods: an array of copper rings and beads was brought up by bucket and pulley and laid out on the sand.

The people of al Fau used the pre-Arabic script known as Musnad al Jenoubi. Behind the city a number of inscriptions and graffiti have been found on the rocks of the Tuwaiq escarpment. The most striking of these is the 10 m. high representation of the god Kahl worshipped there at one time. He has a dagger at his waist and two huge spears by his side.

The works of art found in al Fau include some lovely little bronze figurines of Hellenistic design but showing Egyptian and Assyrian influences. There are artefacts of alabaster and glass and frescoes and a quantity of pottery known as al Fau ware. They are all housed in the University's Department of Archaeology and can be seen there by appointment. Thursday mornings are reserved for women.

Bronze dolphin from Qaryat al Fau.

DIRECTIONS

Take **Route 10** south to Sulayyil, about 580 km from central Riyadh. SET YOUR ODOMETER AT **0**. After about 40 km turn left on the road to Sharourah. At about 110 km you will see on your left a clump of trees which marks the excavation mound There is at this point, also on your left, a restaurant called the Qaryat al Fau beside a petrol station. Turn off the road and make for the trees. There you will find the entrance gate and a guard.

You will need 4 wheel-drive for the 1 km from the road to the site.

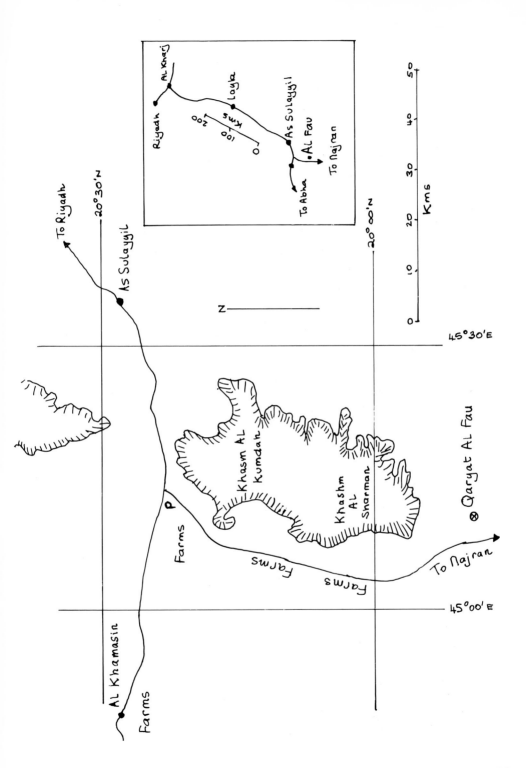

31 Wahba Crater

THREE DAY TRIP MINIMUM

4 WHEEL DRIVE

One of the most spectacular sights in Arabia, the Wahba crater is a 3 km wide circle of white sunk into the black 'harrah' (old lava flows) north-east of Taif. Although 700 km from Riyadh this is well worth the effort. The crater sides plunge 700 feet below ground level, a breath-taking sight (and a heart-stopping moment if you approach at dusk, as there is no warning of the rim's edge.)

It is not known whether the crater was formed by a meteorite impact or by volcanic activity, in the form of an underground explosion. Most people accept the latter theory though there is no lava or volcanic debris on the crater's rim. There is a source of underground water which bubbles up through the surface just below the rim on the north side, forming pools and a charming little palm garden. Around the pools there is thick growth of grass and palms, and in the muddy water frogs and tiny green leeches. The air is full of the sound of bulbuls and you have the sudden flash of sunbirds as they make their tiny nests in the acacia trees nearby.

The descent to the crater bottom and the climb back up is quite gruelling on a hot day, so be prepared with water and hats. It is best made through the palm grove. The crater centre is covered in a white crystalline substance.

Camping sites are easy to find, on one of the ledges overlooking the crater: it is wonderful to wake in the morning to the view down on to the white centre. It is possible to walk round most of the rim: the whole circumference is about 11 km. Look out for little glittering pieces of black obsidian and semi-precious green peridots, both formed in volcanic action.

In the desert to the north and east of the crater you can see the old lava flows with the ripples still visible and the edges where the lava cooled and the flow stopped. This could be relatively recent volcanic activity: we know of a volcanic eruption in 1256 AD which stopped just short of Medina.

About 20 km north-north-east of the crater by car is a 3 km long lake, an unexpected sight in that barrenness. The lake is surrounded by a wooded area of acacia trees and bushes and the calm, rather muddy water is full of little triops.

The crater.

The pool north of the crater.

DIRECTIONS

Take the New Makkah Road west, (**Route 40 W**). SET YOUR ODOMETER AT **0** as you pass the main entrance to the Diplomatic Quarter.

Go through Zalim.

At 636 km turn right at the sign for Maran, Umoldom (Um A'doom) and Dughaib. RE-SET YOUR ODOMETER AT **0**.

After 44 km turn left at a T-junction. At 47 kms in the village of Mushrif, turn right.

At 48 km turn left. The tarmac ends at 50 km.

Continue along the track to al Hofr (Haffar) which is reached at 80 km. Here you will find petrol. Continue past al Hofr to the crater, at 86.5 km.

Go round to the north side to find the shelf which is ideal for camping.

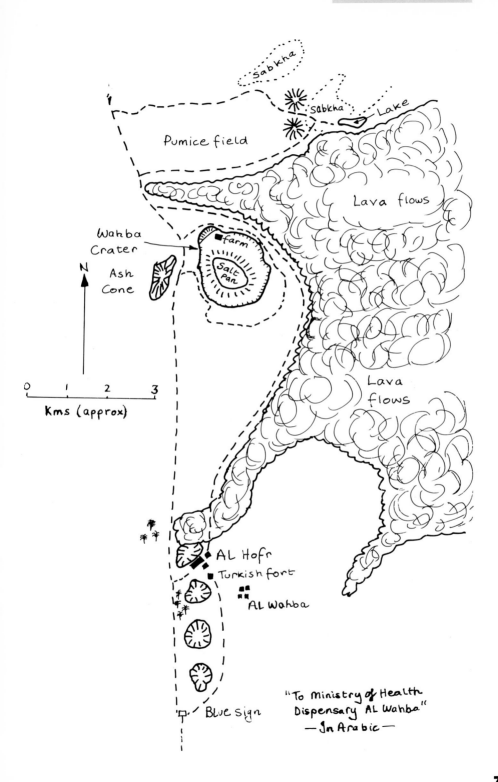

Sabkha

Sabkha

Lake

Pumice field

Lava flows

Wahba Crater

Ash Cone

N

farm

Salt Pan

Lava flows

0 1 2 3

Kms (approx)

AL Hofr

Turkish fort

AL Wahba

Blue sign

"To Ministry of Health
Dispensary AL Wahba"
— In Arabic —

TRAVEL DOCUMENTS AND ANTIQUITY SITES

You will need a travel letter signed by your sponsor to take trips outside Riyadh. It is best to have one which is valid for all parts of the Kingdom.

To visit some archaeological sites in this book, permission is required from the Department of Antiquities and Museums in Shamaisy Street. The sites are:

- Abu Jifan fort
- Medain Saleh (Al Hijr) and the railway station at al Hijr
- al Fau in Wadi Dawasir
- al Uqair in the Eastern Province

Either visit the Museum personally, or write to the Director-General, Department of Antiquities and Museums, PO Box 3734, Riyadh 11481. Tel. 411 5777, ext. 233.

Permission takes at least two weeks to obtain by post. A personal visit may speed the process. You will need to supply the following:

- A formal letter of application signed by the applicant's sponsor.
- Name, nationality and passport number of every passenger, and the number of cars.
- The proposed date of visit and duration of stay at the site.

Please respect the natural history of the Kingdom. Do not damage vegetation or kill wild animals. When visiting an archaeological site, do not remove artefacts and be very careful not to damage the remains.

Take only memories: leave only footprints

Key to maps on pages 76-85

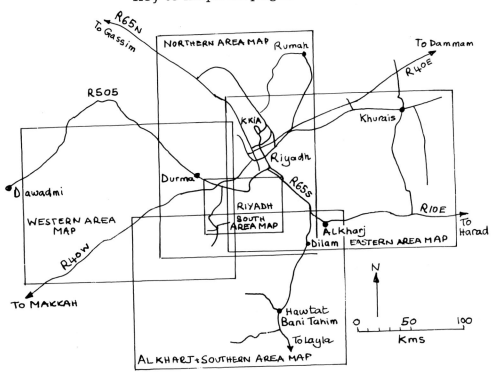

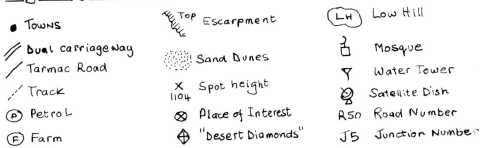

Key To Symbols used in Maps

- ● Towns
- // Dual carriageway
- / Tarmac Road
- ⁄⁄ Track
- Ⓟ Petrol
- Ⓕ Farm

- TOP Escarpment
- Sand Dunes
- X 1104 Spot height
- ⊗ Place of Interest
- ⊕ "Desert Diamonds"

- LH Low Hill
- Mosque
- Water Tower
- Satellite Dish
- R50 Road Number
- J5 Junction Number

Maps *The National Guide and Atlas of the Kingdom of Saudi Arabia* (Zaki Farsi) is widely available and gives up-to-date coverage of the road system and plenty of geographical and other useful information. Make sure you have the edition with 134 pages of sectional maps. The summary edition is not useful for our purposes.

The Kingdom's highways are now being officially numbered and where available the handbook refers to them. The figures on the ground are often only in Arabic and may sometimes lag behind the official gazetting of numbers.

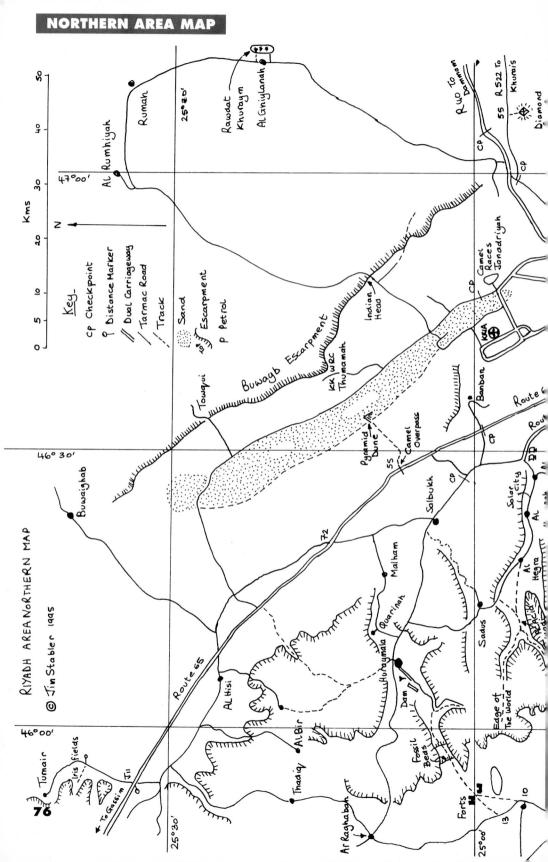

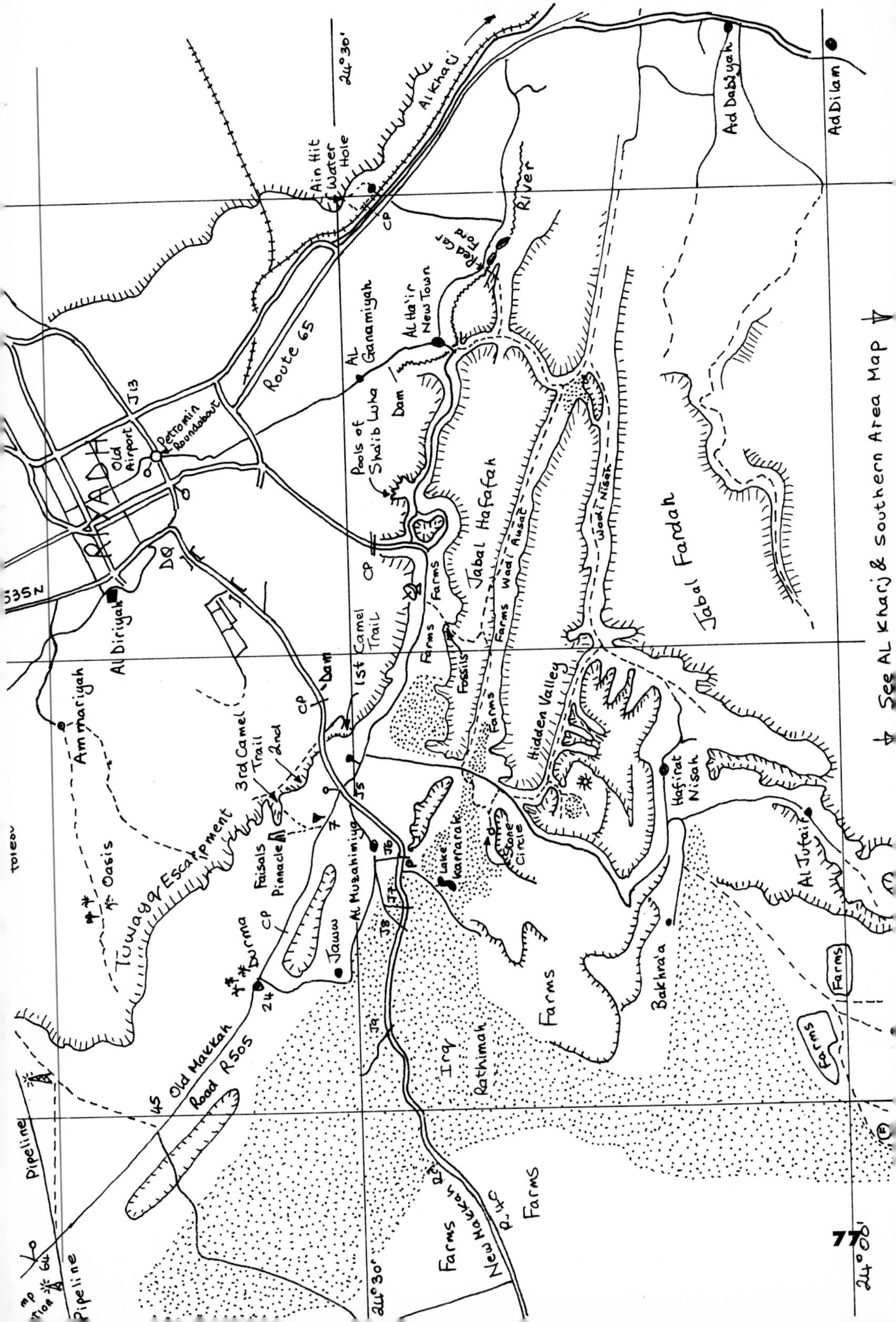

Ad Dilam

Ad Dabiyah

Al Khadi

24°30'

Ain Hit Water Hole

CP

Red Car Ford

River

Route 65

AL Ganamiyah

Al Ha'ir New Town

Dam

Pools of Shu'ib Luha

Old Airport J13

Petromin Roundabout

RIYADH

Jabal Hafafah

Jabal Fardah

535N

CP

Farms

Wadi Awsat

Wadi Nisah

Fossils

Al Diriyah

DQ

Am mariyah

Oasis

Dam

1st Camel Trail

CP
2nd

3rd Camel Trail

Faisals Pinnacle

Burma

CP

Jauw

Al Musahmiyah

35

76

J8

77

Stone Circle

Hidden Valley

Hafirat Nisah

Al Jufair

Tuwaig Escarpment

24

45 Old Makkah Road R505

Lake Kaarara

Iraq Rathimah

New Makkah R 40 Rd

Farms

Farms

Bakhra

Farms

Farms

Farms

Pipeline

TO EOV

Pipeline

map & tion A

Pipeline

24°30'

24°08'

→ See AL Kharj & Southern Area Map ▽

77'

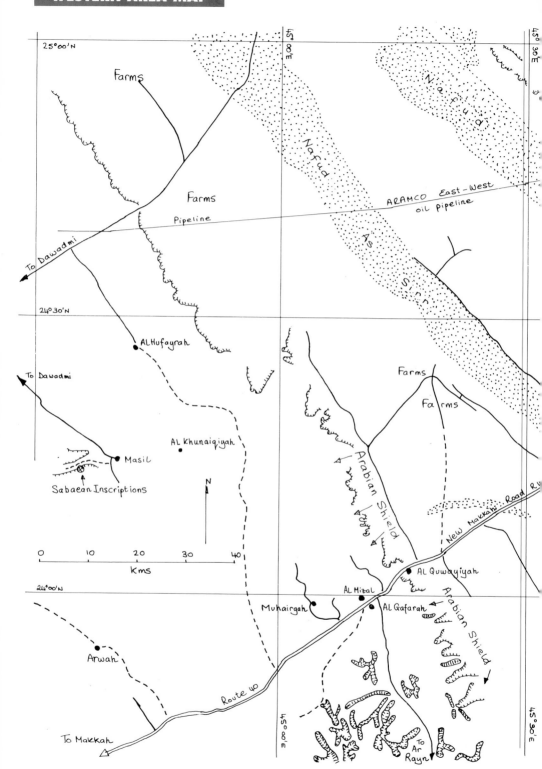

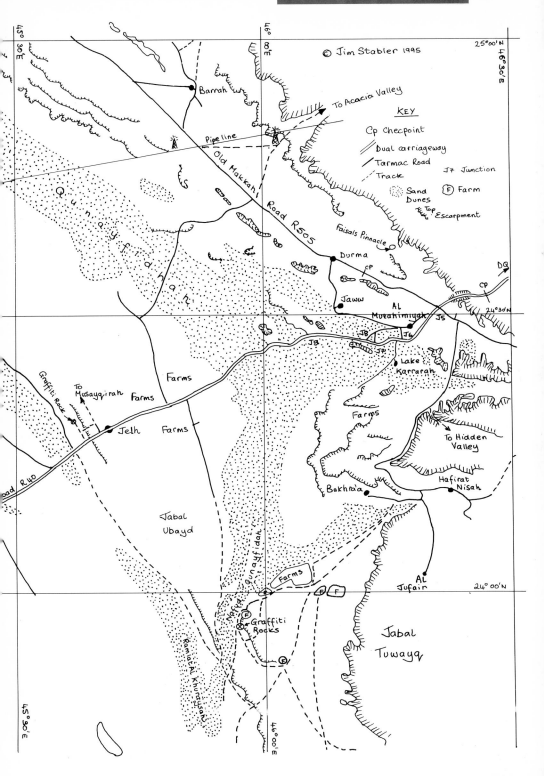

© Jim Stabler 1995

KEY

Cp Checpoint
⫽ Dual carriageway
┬ Tarmac Road
⋯ Track
Jʒ Junction
Ⓕ Farm
Sand Dunes
Top Escarpment

To Acacia Valley

Barnah

Pipe line

Qunayfidhah

Old Makkah Road R505

Faisals Pinnacle

Durma   Cp   DQ
                Cp
Jaww   Al
        Muzahimiyah   Js   24°30'N
        J8   J6
    J9   J7

Lake Karrarah

Farms

To Musayqirah   Farms
Farms
Graffiti Rock
Jelh   Farms

To Hidden Valley

Road R40

Hafirat Nisah

Bakhra

Jabal Ubayd

Wadi Qunayfidah

Farms
Ⓕ
Ⓕ Graffiti Rocks

Al Jufain   24°00'N

Ramlat Al Khuraysa

Jabal Tuwayq

Ⓕ

45°30'E

46°00'E

25°00'N 46°30'E

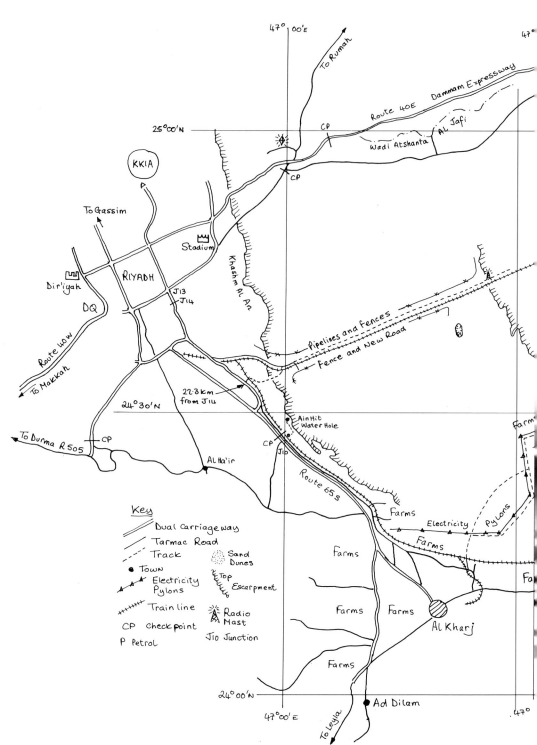

Key

- Dual carriageway
- Tarmac Road
- Track
- Town
- Electricity Pylons
- Train line
- CP Checkpoint
- P Petrol
- Sand Dunes
- Top Escarpment
- Radio Mast
- J10 Junction

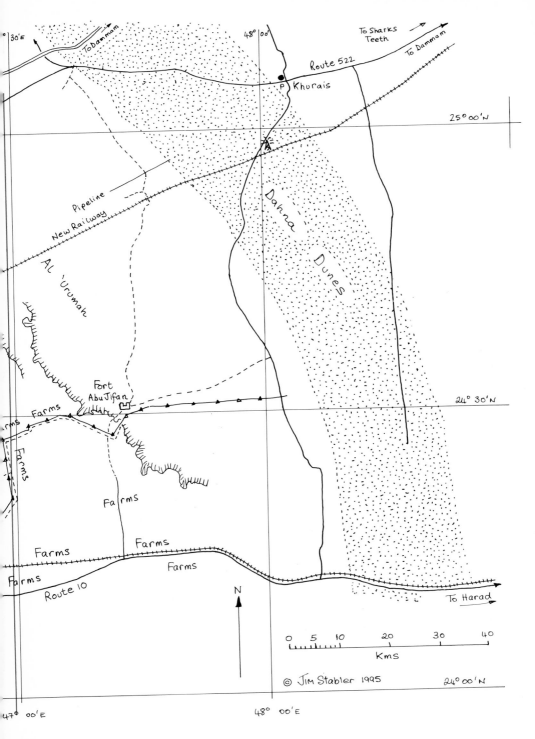

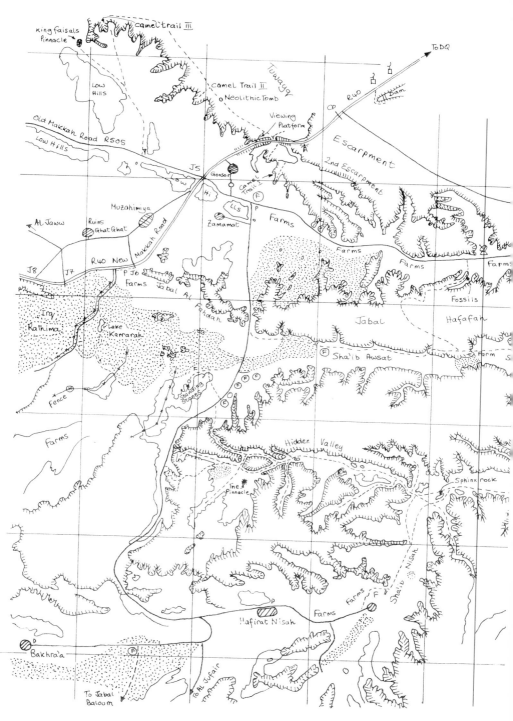

DQ

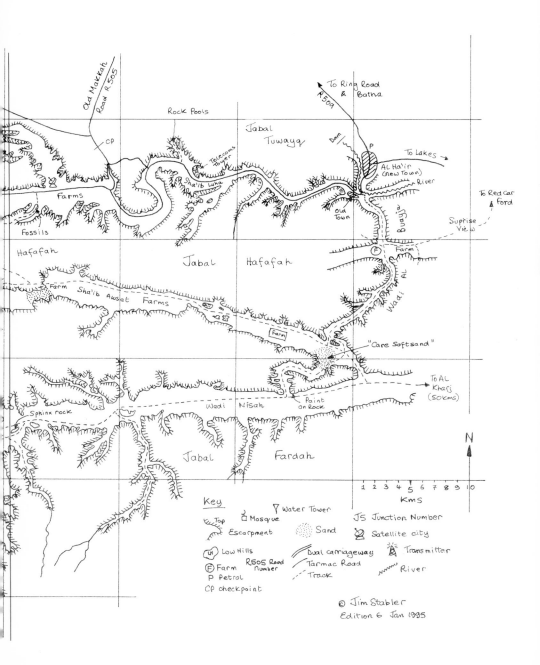

Key

- Top — Escarpment
- (LH) Low Hills
- (F) Farm
- R505 Road Number
- P Petrol
- CP checkpoint
- Mosque
- Sand
- Dual carriageway
- Tarmac Road
- Track
- Water Tower
- JS Junction Number
- Satellite city
- Transmitter
- River

© Jim Stabler
Edition 6 Jan 1995

1 2 3 4 5 6 7 8 9 10
Kms

N

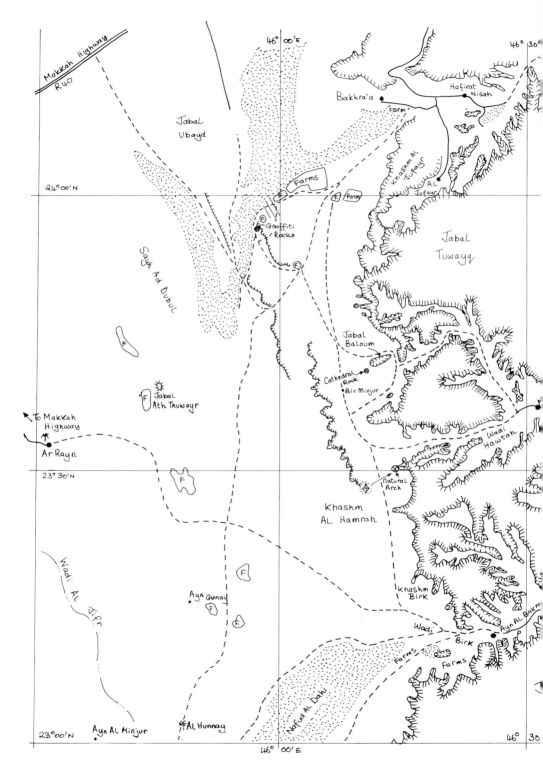

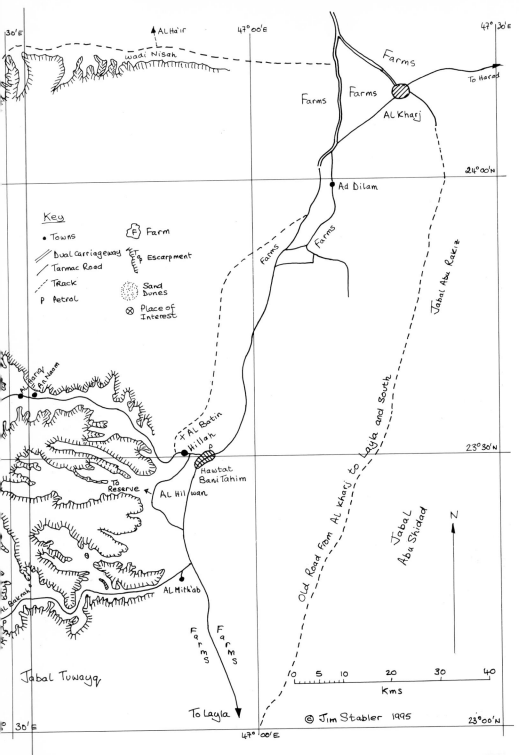

Key

Towns
Dual carriageway
Tarmac Road
Track
P   Petrol

F   Farm
Escarpment
Sand Dunes
⊗   Place of Interest

AL Ha'ir
Wadi Nisah
Farms
Farms
Farms
Al Kharj
To Harad
24° 00'N
Ad Dilam
Farms
Farms
Jabal Abu Rakiz
Al Aariq
Ain Naam
Al Batin
Hillah
23° 30'N
Hawtat Bani Tahim
To Reserve
Al Hilwan
Old Road From Al Kharj to Layla and South
Jabal Aba Shidad
N
Al Bakrah
Al Mith'ab
Jabal Tuwayq
Farms Farms

0   5   10   20   30   40
Kms

To Layla
© Jim Stabler 1995
23° 00'N

30'E
47° 00'E
47° 30'E
30'E
47° 00'E

ACKNOWLEDGEMENTS

I would like to thank: Vernon Cassin, who contributed the article on the Sharks' Teeth site near Khurais, Michele Judzewitsch, Clara Semple and Patricia Barbor, who kindly did the black-and-white sketches. The following friends provided colour photographs: Michele Judzewitsch, Kevin Dunham of the King Khalid Wildlife Research Centre, Jane Lewis, and William Facey.

I am very grateful, also, to the following friends who have helped provide and check information for this handbook: Hatoun al Fassi, Marcelle and Douglas Stobie, Sibella and Stuart Laing, Alessandro de Maigret, Peter Harrigan, William Facey, Kevin Dunham, Richard Kempf, Seija and Tapio Leino, Ray Tyson, Doris and Harro Lorenzen, Sir Alan Munro, John and Pamela Bunney, Brigadier Nick Hepworth, and, of course, my husband, Andrew Thompson, who took me everywhere and checked everything.

SOURCES

Prof. A.R. Al-Ansari: *Qaryat al-Fau, a Portrait of Pre-Islamic Civilisation in Saudi Arabia*, University of Riyadh, 1982.

ATLAL: *The Journal of Saudi Arabian Archaeology*, Department of Antiquities and Museums, Ministry of Education, Riyadh, 1977-Present.

Sheila Collenette: *An Illustrated Guide to the Flowers of Saudi Arabia*, Scorpion Publishing Ltd., London, 1985.

The Desert Ramblers: *Desert Rambles, an Anthology of Desert Ramblers' Trips 1978-1981*, reproduced privately in Riyadh.

William Facey: *Riyadh, the Old City*, Immel Publishing, London 1992.

Cyril Glassé: *The Concise Encyclopaedia of Islam*, Stacey International, London, 1989.

P.A.D. Hollom, R.F. Porter, S. Christensen & Ian Willis: *Birds of the Middle East and North Africa*, T. & A.D. Poyser, Staffs., England, 1988.

Betty Lipscombe-Vincett: *Wild Flowers of Central Saudi Arabia*, Betty Lipscombe-Vincett.

Don and Betty Minden: *Desert Drifters*, Don and Betty Minden, Riyadh, 1986.

Jill Silsby: *Inland Birds of Saudi Arabia*, Immel Publishing, London, 1980.